MAKING OF THE INDIAN
CONSTITUTION

SHRADDHA VERMA

TRUE SIGN
PUBLISHING HOUSE

Published by True Sign Publishing House
Address: SY. No. 21/2 & 21/3, Sonnenahalli,
Krishnarajapura, Bengaluru,
Karnataka - 560049 India
E-mail: truesignbooks@gmail.com
Website: www.truesign.in

Making Of The Indian Constitution

Author: Shraddha Verma

ISBN: 978-93-5584-983-0

First Edition: 2023

CONTENTS

Making of the Indian Constitution

Introduction:

The Constituent Assembly framed the Constitution of India and the demand for this was proposed for the first time in India in 1934. But again this demand was put forward by the Indian National Congress, with a resolution passed in Faizpur session on 28th December, 1936. Jawaharlal Nehru, in 1938, demanded for the Constituent Assembly consequently: "The National Congress stands for an independent and democratic state. It has proposed that the Constitution of free India must be framed, by a Constituent Assembly elected on the basis of adult franchise." In November 1939, after the resignation of the Congress ministries they again demanded for the Constituent Assembly. But the British resisted this demand till the starting of World War II, after that they understood the urgency to resolve this problem. In the year March 1942, Sir Stafford Cripps, brought the proposal to the British government with a draft declaration that would be agreed by them if both the major parties like Congress and Muslim League came with an understanding, such as,

1. The Indian constitution must be framed by an elected Constituent Assembly of the people of India;

2. The Constitution must provide the status of dominion to India, equal partnership of the British Commonwealth Nations;

3. There must be one Indian Union consisting of all the Provinces and Indian States; but

4. Any state or province who do not want to accept the constitution would be free to have its own constitutional position, for with such provinces British government may enter with distinct constitutional provisions.

The two parties did not come to an understanding to agree with the proposal, and the Muslim League insisted that:

- India must be divided into two independent states on communal lines, and some of the provinces embarked by Jinnah must form a separate Muslim state.

- In the place of one Constituent Assembly there must be two assemblies.

The Constituent Assembly which was set up depending upon the recommendations of the Cabinet Mission Plan was to frame the constitution of Republic India. On 9th December, 1946, the Constituent Assembly met to start the important mission to draft the constitution of independent India. Though the body of the Constituent Assembly was not a sovereign body but it had to frame the constitution within the guidelines of the Mission Plan. It had to observe the honor and the commitments of the British who were about to leave with regard to the minorities and Indian states. The draft which they made had to be accepted by the British so that it could get the stamp of British.

The province or the state of India were allocated seats depending upon their representation in the assemblies, with this they had to select 292 members from these constituencies, with a maximum of 92 seats to a state. The seats were allocated among the main communities, depending upon their representation and there were 210, general constituencies, 78 for Muslims, 8 for Sikhs, and 3 seats were allocated to Chief Commissioner's provinces and 1 to British Baluchistan. Each community elected their own representatives, by a single transferable vote. The constitution had to decide the way of election of representation of Indian states. On December 9th, 1946 the Constituent Assembly was formed. The Muslim league did not take part in the discussions because of its separate demand.

Formation of the Constituent Assembly:

Dr. Rajendra Prasad was elected as the permanent president of the Constituent Assembly, it adopted the objectives resolution moved by Jawaharlal Nehru on 22nd January, 1947 and it was, "The objective of the framers of the Constitution was declared to be the creation of a Sovereign Republic of India; unanimous approval was given to another resolution moved by Nehru recommending a redistribution of the provinces so as to make them 'homogeneous units based on linguistic, cultural, administrative and economic considerations' as soon as possible the new Constitution had been enforced". This was adopted in the second plenary session. In the third plenary session from April 28th to May 2nd, it discussed about the Fundamental Rights, which was submitted by the Union Powers

Committee and Advisory Committee. The committee firstly decided to give powers such as, defense, foreign affairs, communications, finance and assortment powers to the Union Cabinet, but later the second committee had divided the fundamental powers into two types, like justifiable and non-justifiable rights and also included that the Fundamental Rights must be equal for all the persons irrespective of religion, caste, race and sex. Despite the fact that castes are divided into scheduled caste/tribes, backward classes, and generally, no one should be discriminated against. It also confirmed that "no title shall be conferred by the union and no citizen of the union shall accept any title from a foreign state". It was decided after a proposal from Dr. Rajendra Prasad, that the constitution must be written both in Hindustani and English hence, the Assembly was adjourned sine die. Later, it met again and deliberated three important subjects like:

1. Report of the Union Constitution Committee on the proposed constitution

2. The report of a model Constitution for the Province was reported and

3. Adoption of Indian National Flag. On the midnight of 14th August a meeting was held by the Constituent Assembly for the transfer of powers to India. The fourth meeting during August 20-29 recommended:

   - The Federal and Provincial powers accepted the report of second Union Powers Committee,

   - The report given by the Advisory Committee on Minorities, which inter alia, provided for the elimination of the former communal electorates and was substituted by the joint electorates and

   - The Constituent Assembly for its future working for the constitution and law-making body. This report suggested that the constitution and law-making must be done on separate days in separate sessions by the Constituent Assembly. It was also stated that Constituent Assembly functioned as dominion legislature must be presided over by the Speaker and Ministers had the right to involve in the constitution making, they had the right to vote till they became the members. It was recommended that the members of the princely states will also involve in this process.

   - The Constituent Assembly adopted a resolution on 29th August to form a Drafting Committee, to prepare the constitution by considering all the sessions given by the different committees. It

 MAKING OF THE INDIAN CONSTITUTION

was directed to observe certain matters of the 1935, Government Act of India. Dr. BR Ambedkar was the chairman of the committee. The Drafting Committee was submitted a draft constitution on 21st February, 1948 and it was discussed in the assembly and it was accepted on 26th November, 1949 but it came into act from 26th January, 1950. For making this task successful it took 1965 days, and out of these days 114 days were taken for considering the draft constitution and there were 11 meetings held to make this task. But there were some other articles to the constitution such as, citizenship, elections, provisional parliament, temporary and transitional powers which came into force on 26th January, 1949.

- During the debates of the assembly, Congress always dominated and they took the lead and they flourished to carry out their thoughts.

- There was an argument that, there was no proper opposition to the Congress in the Constituent Assembly so that they could condemn the ideas which were not good for the constitution, hence, the opinions were not sufficiently presented.

- In the Constituent Assembly most of them were from the lawyer turned politicians therefore, the constitution was mostly with the views of them and it happened to be tailored by lawyers.

- It was also argued that when the constitution was prepared the people were not been asked for their acceptance. Whatever, argued by them was in fact a reality, the Constituent Assembly was not elected on the grounds of adult franchise and it cannot be regarded as the true representative body. But at the same time one had to accept that Congress had taken best possible efforts to bring this constitution with most efficient personalities which were present at that time. The election of the candidates to the assembly was done on the communal grounds, only Muslims and Sikhs were given such opportunity. The Congress also gave preference to the candidates from the scheduled caste, Anglo-Indian community, Christians, Viceroy's executive council, former members of the legislatives from the provinces, industrial person, and medical professionals, etc. It was a fact that all the discussions were dominated by the Congress and its members, and it was due to this fact that the Congress fought for the freedom of the country and it was the party which was accepted by most of the people. But it can be observed that it never guided its own personal interest in it, it did not put its own personal agendas in it, it had been always looked for which was the best for the country at that point of time. Commenting about this, Prof. Rao says that, "though made by the Congress party, the Constitution does not contain even a single article that favoured the party at the expense of other parties." The critiques which were mentioned was not submitted for referendum, even though it was correct but it did not have any importance. It fact the first general election which were held in 1952, were itself regarded as the referendum to the constitution, and it can be noted that people had given its acceptance to it. The candidates who stated that they would scrap this constitution and frame a better one, were defeated in that election. This instance was an indicator that the majority of the people had accepted the constitution.

The Assembly was adjourned sine die. Later, it met again and deliberated three important subjects. The Constituent Assembly adopted a resolution on 29th August, to form a drafting committee, Dr. BR Ambedkar was the chairman of the committee. The drafting committee submitted a draft constitution on 21st February, 1948.and it was discussed in the assembly and it was accepted on 26th November, 1949 but it came into act from 26th January, 1950. Since the inception of the Constituent Assembly, an argument was there about its representativeness.

Basic Foundation of the Indian Constitution

Introduction:

The Indian constitution drafted by the Constituent Assembly submitted its draft constitution on 21st February, 1948 and it was finally accepted on 26th November, 1949 but it came into existence on 26th January, 1950. The Constitution of India was a very virtuous document and it could be considered as the fundamental law of the country, hence, it would have an important position in the structure of the political system in the country. The makers of the constitution were the most intelligent and they made a constitution which was suited to the nation. To prepare this constitution they had gone through all the constitutions in the world and most of the provisions were borrowed from other nations. The Chairman of the drafting committee, Dr. Ambedkar, witnessed as, "One likes to ask whether there can be anything new in a constitution framed at this hour in the history of the world. More than hundred years have rolled by when the first written constitution was drafted. It has then been followed by many other countries reducing their constitution to writings... Given these facts, all constitutions in their main provision must look similar. The only new things if there be any in a constitution framed so late in the day or the variations made to remove the faults to accommodate it to the needs of the country....."

Gandhian Thoughts:

These principle were based on the thoughts of Gandhi:

1. State must take necessary steps to systematize village panchayats and provide them with powers so that they can perform as the units of self-government; (Art 40)

2. The state must deliver early childhood care, economic interest and education to the weaker sections; (Art 45)

3. State must encourage the cottage industries of individual or in groups in rural areas; (Art 43)

4. State must deliver and promote the agriculture and animal husbandry, and prevent the slaughtering of cows and other mulching animals; (Art 48)

5. State must improve the public health and prohibit the intoxicating drugs and drinks; (Art 47).

American and other Countries Judicial Review: The concept of individual judiciary from the USA constitution, from Canada the Federal aspects, Directive Principles from Ireland, from South African Constitution, election of Rajya Sabha members and amendments to the constitution and concurrent list in our Constitution is from the Australian Constitution. The most important Act of 1935, Government of India Act has influenced the Indian Constitution most, and most significant feature of our constitution is that the makers of the Constitution has given preference to those principles which are found to be successful and they did not consider those which are founded faulty.

Sources from the Acts of the Government of India:

The Parliament of the British had made Acts in the years of 1909, 1919 and 1935. The most significant act was made in 1935, Government of India Act, The British Parliament also made an act for the independence of India as well. The Act of 1935 had a significance in the preparation of the Indian constitution, it can be said that the constitution of India is the replica of the Government of India Act 1935, according to Prof. Jennings, "The consultation derives directly from the Government India Act 1935 from which in fact, many of its provisions are copied almost textually." The Constitution of India, in fact opted for the dispersal of powers, it recommended for the federal type of organization at the centre, self-rule to the states, bicameral system at centre and in some of the states, the discretionary and emergency powers to Governors and Governor-Generals, these powers actually altered to meet the requirements of the changing times.

Sources from the Parliamentary System of Britain:

It was observed that the British parliamentary system was influenced by the makers of the constitution of India. It was evident that the long relationship with Britain also had to be considered and the makers would very much know about the existent law in the country and it would be one reason to select the parliamentary system of government to India. In fact, the Indian parliamentary system also worked as similar to that of British system. It could be seen at the centre and the state, the one who was elected by the elected representatives would be responsible for the legislation. The President of India who was the head of the nation but he was a nominal head just like that of British Queen or King. In the real sense the head of the nation was the Prime Minister. There were certain similarities between them, for instance the minister must be from either of the house, if not /he has to be elected within six months' time. The makers of the constitution in India not only hired the parliamentary system from Britain but also hired the convention in regard to the parliament system as well. There was similarity between the two members of the parliament, The Indian members had the same sort of privileges like that of British members of Parliament. The important ideologies which were borrowed from them were Rule of Law, and the patterns of the Lower House over the Upper House were mostly common like that of Britain.

Sources and their Impact on the Constitution:

The process of constitution was the result of regular improvements, hence, when the makers of the constitution prepared the constitution they looked for such improvements which were most suitable in the prevailing situations. That was the reason they did not evade to use such principles which were used in the countries like USA, German, Ireland, South Africa, etc. in their constitution. It was observed that they did not select those principles which were proved to be faulty and of defective nature. If we

    Making Of The Indian Constitution

observe the Fundamental Rights of Indian constitution it is almost similar to that of United Sates Bill of Rights, in the case of judicial system they took the concept of their independent judicial system. The functions of the Vice President of America, we adopted and incorporated in our constitution. The federal structure which we have in our constitution is nothing but it was from the Canadian Constitution. At the same time we had borrowed the idea of Directive Principles from the Irish Republic, and other ideas such as the nomination of the President to Rajya Sabha like, people from fields of science, culture, social service, etc. were imprints of the Irish Constitution. The election to the members of Rajya Sabha and the amendments to the constitution was from the South African Constitution, the concurrent list was from the Australian Constitution.

Debates in the Constituent Assembly:

The debates which occurred in the assembly were of use for the makers of the constitution, they had discussed every component of the constitution very systematically and different ways and means for that particular aspect were debated. These debates made them to get more information and made them to make constitution more effectively. Along with this the critiques which they received also made them to rectify their faults in that particular principle.

Preamble and the Philosophy of the Constitution

Every constitution contains the preamble, with its objectives, it is the opening statement during the speech or writings Dyer talks about the preamble as, "key to open the minds of the people, makers of the Act, and the mischief's which they intended to redress." The most important work which was done by the Constituent Assembly was they prepared the objectives and those principles which guide the constitution. There were eight objectives in total.

1. This Constituent Assembly declares its firm and solemn resolve to proclaim India as an independent Sovereign Republic and to draw up for her future governance a Constitution:`

2. WHEREIN the territories that now comprise British India, the territories that now form the Indian States, and such other parts of India as are outside British India and the States as well as such other territories as are willing to be constituted into the Independent Sovereign India shall be a Union of them all; and

3. WHEREIN the said territories, whether with their present boundaries or with such others as may be determined by the Constituent Assembly and thereafter according to law of the Constitution shall possess and retain the status of autonomous units, together with residuary powers, and exercise all powers and functions of government and administration, save and except such powers and functions as are vested in or assigned to the Union, or as are inherent or implied in the Union or resulting therefrom, and

4. WHEREIN all power and authority of the Sovereign Independent India, its constituent parts and organs of government, are derived from the people; and

5. WHEREIN shall be guaranteed and secured ;to all the people of India justice, social, economic, and political; equality of status, of opportunity, and before the law; freedom of thought, expression, belief, faith, worship, vocation, association and action, subject to law and public morality; and

6. WHEREIN adequate safeguards shall be provided for minorities, backward and tribal areas, and depressed and other backward classes; and

7. WHEREBY shall be' maintained the integrity of the territory of the Republic and its sovereign rights on land, sea and air according to justice and the law of civilized nations; and

8. this ancient land attain its rightful and honoured place in the world -and make its full and willing contribution to the promotion of world peace and the welfare of mankind.

Along with the objective resolution the philosophy of the Constitution which confined in the preamble to the Constitution as follows:

"WE, THE PEOPLE OF INDIA, having resolved to constitute India into a SOVEREIGN DEMOCRATIC REPBLIC and to secure to all its citizens; JUSTICE, social economic and political; LIBERTY, of thought, expression, belief, faith and worship. EQUALITY of status and opportunity, and promote among them all; FRATERNITY assuring the dignity of the individual and the unity of the Nation; IN OUR CONSTITUENT ASSEMBLY this twenty sixth day of November 1949, do HEREBY ADOPT, ENACT AND GIVE OURSELVES THIS CONSTITUTION."

The Preamble as Amended by the 42nd Amendment:

On 18th December the 42nd Amendment came into force in the Preamble to the constitution: (a) For the words, 'SOVEREIGN DEMOCRATIC REPUBLIC', the words, 'SOVEREIGN SOCIALIST SECULAR REPUBLIC' shall be substituted ; and (b) For the words, "Unity of the Nation", the words unity and integrity of the "Nation" shall be substituted. So the preamble as amended reads as follows:

WE, THE PEOPLE OF INDIA, having solemnly resolved to constitute India into a SOVEREIGN SOCIALIST SECULAR DEMOCRATIC REPUBLIC and to secure to all its citizens:

JUSTICE, social, economic and political; LIBERTY of thought, expression, belief, faith and worship;

EQUALITY of status and of opportunity; and to promote among them all FRATERNITY assuring the dignity of the individual and the unity and integrity of the Nation;

IN OUR CONSTITUENT ASSEMBLY this twenty-sixth day of November, 1949, do HEREBY ADOPT, ENACT AND GIVE TO OURSELVES THIS CONSTITUTION

The 44th amendment and other amendments did not change in the preamble and hence, India continues to remain SOVEREIGN SOCIALIST DEMOCRATIC SECULAR REPUBLIC.

Sovereignty: In the year 1947, the Independence Act stated India a Dominion with the Queen of England as the Head of the State. This was designed by the people of India by their representatives assembled in the sovereign Constituent Assembly to regulate the prospect of the country politically. Thus the words, "WE the people of India, Adopt, Enact and Give ourselves this Constitution" hence, it states the eventual sovereignty of the people.

Republican Democracy: Democratic republic means that sovereignty remains with the people they show their sovereignty through the parliament at the centre and by the legislature in the states and the representatives are elected on the grounds of the adult franchise; the executive is accountable to it. The fundamental rights are the most important rights in the democratic structure. India is regarded as a Republic hence, there is no question of hereditary selection in the governmental process.

Political Justice: Political justice means that all the citizens must have equal political rights. Right to vote is the significant right of the political rights, though there were dissimilarities. For this right the makers gave the opportunity that every citizen have the right to participate in the political system of the country. Hence, they recommended for the universal adult franchise without any qualification was adopted. Every five years the representatives must be elected by the adult people, therefore, constitution guarantees the political justice.

Economic Justice: In the preamble another important right given was economic justice. To secure this right constitution provided the following principles in the Directive Principles of State Policy in Chapter IV to be followed by the state:

- All the citizens have the right to an adequate means of livelihood;

- The ownership and control of the material resources of the community are to be so distributed as best to subserve the common good;

- The operation of the economic system does not result in the concentration of wealth and the means of production to the common detriment;

- There is to be equal pay for equal work;

- The health and strength of the workers is not abused and citizens are not forced by economic necessity to enter avocations (Manual Workers) unsuited to their age and strength;

- Children are given opportunities to develop in a healthy manner and in condition of freedom and dignity, and childhood and youth are protected against exploitation and against material and moral deprivation.

Social Justice: The constitution of India, guarantees the social justice as well.

Which means that the democracy must be protracted to the social provinces, it must have the concept of equality, liberty, and fraternity. It also abolishes un-touchability and assures the cultural safeguard to minorities.

Liberty: In the system of democracy, liberty is one of the spirit, without this right the democracy cannot be thought of, this was preserved in the preamble, it assures liberty of thought, expression, faith, belief and worship.

These rights are assured in the State by Part III of the constitution, subject of course to the implementation of Directive Principles for the common good and fundamental duties.

Equality: In the preamble it assured the equality of opportunity and status. It safeguards the same in the constitution by the following provisions:

1. The state shall not deny to any person equality before the laws or the equal protection of the laws within the territory of India.

2. The state shall not discriminate on the grounds of religion, race, sex, place of birth or any of them.

3. There shall be equality of opportunity for all citizens in matters relating to employment or appointment to any office under the state. No citizen on the grounds of the religion, sex, race, caste, descent, place of birth, residence or any of them, be ineligible, or discriminated against in respect of any employment or office under the state.

4. Untouchability is abolished and its practice in any form is forbidden.

Fraternity: This protects the integrity and unity of the nation, to safe-guard this the constitution has provided definite fundamental duties to its citizens, they are:

1. To promote harmony and the spirit of common brotherhood amongst all the people of India transcending religious, linguistic and regional or sectional diversities; to renounce practices derogatory to the dignity of women;

2. To uphold and protect the sovereignty, unity and integrity of India;

3. To defend the country and render national service when called upon to do so.

Dignity of the Individual: The dignity of each individual cannot be observed unless the fraternity is realized, hence, the Preamble states that the State will protect the dignity of each individual, for this reason many Directive Principles have been comprised in Part IV of the constitution, and they are:

1. The state shall direct its policy towards securing that the citizens, men and women, equally have the right to an adequate means to livelihood;

2. The state shall make provision for securing just and humane conditions of work;

3. The state shall endeavour to secure to all workers a living wage, conditions of work ensuring a decent standard of life and full enjoyment of leisure and social and cultural opportunities.

Socialism: After the 42nd constitutional amendment to the constitution the word 'socialist' was inserted in the Preamble which means nationalization of all means of making and the eradication of private property.

Secularism: With the 42nd amendment to the constitution the word 'secularism' was inserted in the Preamble with the Act of 1976, the main ideas of this are as follows:

1. The state does not establish, recognize or endow any religion;

2. It extends full religious freedom to all citizens, the citizens are allowed to follow any religion they like, propagate their religion, change their religion, build and maintain places of worship and other institutions and give religious instructions to their children;

3. The State treats all its citizens as equal before law irrespective of their religious faith, it does not discriminate any citizen in matters of public employment on the grounds of religion, the State does not take the responsibility for the religious or spiritual welfare of its citizens.

Promotion of International Peace: In the ideal of fraternity itself it is embodied in the preamble of the constitution, it is not only for the Indian territories but also has a broader meaning of universal peace and brotherhood. The article 51, of the Constitution states it as:

1. Promote international peace and security;

2. Maintain just and honourable relations between nations;

3. Foster respect for international law and treaty obligations in the dealings of organized peoples with one another;

4. Encourage settlements of international disputes by arbitration.

Conclusion: The basic foundations for the constitution are, the Government of India Acts, of 1909, 1919 and 1935, of all these the act of 1935 is regarded as the most important, they have also taken from the British Parliament system as well. They have also borrowed the principle from other nations like USA, Canada, Italy, German, Irish and South Africa. For making this constitution the discussions during the Constituent Assembly proved to be very helpful. Every constitution has the Preamble, it is the introductory statement in the writings or speeches. There are 8 objectives in the Preamble of the constitution. By the amendment to the 42nd constitution they have inserted certain words in 1976 by an act and it came into force on 18th December, 1976.

Salient Features of the Indian Constitution

Introduction:

The Constituent Assembly framed the constitution and the demand for this came for the first time in India in 1934. But again this demand came forward by the Indian National Congress, with resolution passed in Faizpur session on 28th December, 1936. It submitted its draft constitution on 21st February, 1948 and it was finally accepted on 26th November, 1949 but it came into existence on 26th January, 1950. The Constitution of India is a very virtuous document and it can be considered as the fundamental law of the country, hence, it will have an important position in the structure of the political system in the country. Some of the important salient features of the constitution are as follows:

Written Constitution: The Constitution of India consists of 395 Articles and 8 Schedules in the starting but later they were extended to 12 schedules and the constitution is written. When the Constituent Assembly was formed in 1946 to prepare the Constitution of India, the Constituent Assembly was formed by the representatives from different provinces which were mainly on the communal grounds. They met in New Delhi, in December 1946, and they took almost three years to prepare this Constitution, which was mainly based on their discussions, it was accepted on 26th November, 1949 but it came into force on 26th January, 1950 and from then India became a Republic.

Rigid and Flexible: The Constitution of India is in fact rigid and flexible, which means that, it is rigid because most of its parts cannot be altered or amended by making an ordinary law, and to amend they have to follow either of the three methods which are present in the Constitution. Only some of the facts can be amended by the use of ordinary law-making process in the Parliament. Whereas some of the provision can be amended in the form of Bill and it has to be passed in both the Houses of Parliament by a majority of the total membership of the House and by the majority of not less than two-thirds of the members present and voting; then the bill is sent to the President for his approval. For example, the Bill of Telangana state formation was passed in both the houses before the formation of

Telangana as a separate state. It is also true that there are some other provisions that can be amended by the ratification of the legislature of the States by one-half, then it can be sent to the President for his approval.

Borrowed from Dissimilar Sources: An important and distinguished aspect of the Indian Constitution is that it has borrowed the different principles from different constitutions of the country, they took the best available and those principles which proved to be successful in those countries. For instance, they took the system of Britain's parliament and put same sort of system in our Constitution. The concept of independent judiciary from the USA constitution, from Canada the Federal aspects, Directive Principles from Ireland, from South African Constitution, election of Rajya Sabha members and amendments to the constitution and concurrent list in our Constitution is from the Australian Constitution. The most important Act of 1935, Government of India Act has influenced the Indian Constitution most, and most significant feature of our constitution is that the makers of the Constitution has given preference to those principles which are found to be successful and they did not consider those which are founded faulty.

Comprehensive Administrative Requirements Included:

The Constitution of India is a very big document and it is due to the fact that the constitution was drawn for the Government of India Act, 1935, which is very bulky in nature hence, our Constitution in reality is the replica of the Act of 1935, Government India Act. It was observed by the framers of the Constitution of India primarily Dr. Ambedkar that, with regard to the administration form he found that there is no necessity to change it, but he observed the change is inevitable to the constitution. In it a detailed administrative provisions were included. In the Constitution of India we can see that there is comprehensive provisions about the organs of Judiciary, the Services, the Public Service Commission, Election Commission and the separation of powers between the Centre and the States, etc.

Enclosure of Components of the Constitution:

In the federal states the Constitution is related to the federal government only and the other units of the federation will have to draw separate Constitution of their own. This sort of practice can be observed in the Constitutions of USSR, USA, Canada, and other states of federative forms. But in the case of Indian Constitution, the Constitution of India provided to both the Centre and the States of the Union of India.

Sovereign Democratic Republic:

In the Constitution of India, it is declared that India is Sovereign Democratic Republic, the makers of the Constitution has given this position, in the Indian Independent Act of 1947, it was written India as a dominion of queen of England as the State Head and Governor-General as the representative of the Queen to the State. While preparing the Constitution of India they realized it and they wanted to give full powers and dignity to the nation, hence, in the Preamble of the Constitution they declared India as, Sovereign Democratic Republic. It gives the meaning that India does not owe loyalty to any foreign powers but in fact it is autonomous in all its dealings with other foreign countries and having the similar status in the world community along with other autonomous countries. In the constitution of India it is written that India has the Democracy which means the sovereignty of India lies with the people of India and they are ruled by the elected representatives by the help of adult franchise and the constitution also gives the citizens the fundamental rights as well. In the democratic system we cannot see the presence of hereditary system, even the President of India is elected and the monarchy system which was present before the Independence was totally eradicated. Even though India is Sovereign Republic but it remains with the Commonwealth of Nations with the British monarch as its head, but the status of Indian republic will not be compromised. The Commonwealth Nations are those free and Independent nations and British Monarch is just symbolic head of the association.

Fundamental Rights of the Indian Constitution

Introduction:

The philosophy of democracy is regarded as the rights of the individual and Fundamental Rights provide every individual to lead a happy and better life in the society. The meaning of the Rights was given by Laski as, "are those conditions of the social life without which no man can seek to himself at his best." These rights are considered as the spirit of the constitution, these rights are assured by the Indian Government to its citizens, and these rights are actually borrowed from the Constitution of America.

These fundamental rights in fact protects the liberty of individuals and Directive Principles of State Policy to assure the justice in the areas of politics, social and economic justice to all the citizens.

A complete list of fundamental rights are provided in the Indian Constitution. The six fundamental rights are:

1. Right to Equality (Article 14–18)

2. Right to Freedom (Article 19–22)

3. Right against Exploitation (Article 23–24)

4. Right to Freedom of Religion (Article 25–28)

5. Cultural and Educational Rights (Article 29–30)

6. Right to Constitutional Remedies (Article 32)

The Right to Equality: This is the first Fundamental Right in the Indian Constitution. It is embodied in Articles 14–18, which collectively encompass the general principles of equality before law and non-discrimination and Articles 17–18 which collectively encompass further the philosophy of social equality.

Article 14 guarantees equality before law as well as equal protection of the law to all people within the territory of India. This includes the equal subjection of all persons to the authority of law, as well as equal treatment of persons in similar circumstances. The latter permits the State to classify persons for legitimate purposes, provided there is a reasonable basis for the same, meaning that the classification is required to be non-arbitrary, based on a method of intelligible differentiation among those sought to be classified, as well as have a rational relation to the object sought to be achieved by the classification.

Article 15 prohibits discrimination on the grounds of religion, race, caste, sex, place of birth, and also gender or any of them. This right can be enforced against the State as well as private individuals, with regard to free access to places of public entertainment or places of public resort maintained partly or wholly out of State funds. However, the State is not precluded from making special provisions for women and children or any socially and educationally backward classes of citizens, including the Scheduled Castes and Scheduled Tribes. This exception has been provided since the classes of people mentioned are considered deprived and in need of special protection.

Article 16 guarantees equality of opportunity in matters of public employment and prevents the State from discriminating against anyone in matters of employment on the grounds only of religion, race, caste, sex, descent, place of birth, place of residence or income. It creates exceptions for the implementation of measures of affirmative action for the benefit of any backward class of citizens in order to ensure adequate representation in public service, as well as reservation of an office of any religious institution for a person professing that particular religion.

Article 17 abolishes the practice of untouchability in any form, making it an offense punishable by law. The Protection of Civil Rights Act, 1955 was enacted by Parliament to further this objective.

Article 18 prohibits the State from conferring any titles other than military or academic distinctions, and the citizens of India cannot accept titles from a foreign state. Thus, Indian aristocratic titles and title of nobility conferred by the British have been abolished. However, military and academic distinctions can be conferred on the citizens of India. The awards of Bharat Ratna and Padma Vibhushan can be used by the recipient as a title and do not, accordingly, come within the constitutional prohibition. The Supreme Court, on 15 December 1995, upheld the validity of such awards.

Right to Freedom: The Right to Freedom is covered in Article 19 to 22, with the view of guaranteeing individual rights that were considered vital by the framers of the Constitution, and these Articles also include certain restrictions that may be imposed by the State on individual liberty under specified conditions. Article 19 guarantees six freedoms in the nature of civil rights, which are available only to citizens of India. These include the freedom of speech and expression, freedom of assembly without arms, freedom of association, freedom of movement throughout the territory of our country, freedom to reside and settle in any part of the country of India and the freedom to practice any profession. All these freedoms are subject to reasonable restrictions that may be imposed on them by the State, listed under Article 19 itself. The grounds for imposing these restrictions vary according to the freedom sought to be restricted and include national security, public order, decency and morality, contempt of court, incitement to offences and defamation. The State is also empowered, in the interests of the general public to nationalize any trade, industry or service to the exclusion of the citizens.

The freedoms guaranteed by Article 19 are further sought to be protected by Articles 20–22. The scope of these articles, particularly with respect to the doctrine of due process, was heavily debated by the

Constituent Assembly. It was argued, especially by Benegal Narsing Rau, that the incorporation of such a clause would hamper social legislation and cause procedural difficulties in maintaining order, and therefore it ought to be excluded from the Constitution altogether. The Constituent Assembly in 1948 eventually omitted the phrase "due process" in favor of "procedure established by law". As a result, Article 21, which prevents the encroachment of life or personal liberty by the State except in accordance with the procedure established by law, was, until 1978, construed narrowly as being restricted to executive action. However, in 1978, the Supreme Court in the case of Maneka Gandhi v. Union of India extended the protection of Article 21 to legislative action, holding that any law laying down a procedure must be just, fair and reasonable, and effectively reading due process into Article 21. In the same case, the Supreme Court also ruled that "life" under Article 21 meant more than a mere "animal existence"; it would include the right to live with human dignity and all other aspects which made life "meaningful, complete and worth living." Subsequent judicial interpretation has broadened the scope of Article 21 to include within it a number of rights including those to livelihood, good health, clean environment, water, speedy trial and humanitarian treatment while imprisoned. The right to education at elementary level has been made one of the Fundamental Rights under Article 21A by the 86th Constitutional amendment of 2002. Article 20 provides protection from conviction for offences in certain respects, including the rights against ex post facto laws, double jeopardy and freedom from self-incrimination. Article 22 provides specific rights to arrested and detained persons, in particular the rights to be informed of the grounds of arrest, consult a lawyer of one's own choice, be produced before a magistrate within 24 hours of the arrest, and the freedom not to be detained beyond that period without an order of the magistrate. The Constitution also authorizes the State to make laws providing for preventive detention, subject to certain other safeguards present in Article 22. The provisions pertaining to preventive detention were discussed with scepticism and misgivings by the Constituent Assembly, and were reluctantly approved after a few amendments in 1949. Article 22 provides that when a person is detained under any law of preventive detention, the State can detain such person without trial for only three months, and any detention for a longer period must be authorised by an Advisory Board. The person being detained also has the right to be informed about the grounds of detention, and be permitted to make a representation against it, at the earliest opportunity.

  MAKING OF THE INDIAN CONSTITUTION

Right to Information (RTI)

Right to information has been given the status of a fundamental right under Article 19(1) of the Constitution in 2005. Article 19 (1) under which every citizen has freedom of speech and expression and the right to know how the government works, what roles it plays, what its functions are, and so on.

Right against Exploitation: The Right against Exploitation contained in Articles 23–24, lays down certain provisions to prevent exploitation of the weaker sections of the society by individuals or the State. Article 23 prohibits human trafficking, making it an offence punishable by law, and also prohibits forced labour or any act of compelling a person to work without wages where he was legally entitled not to work or to receive remuneration for it. However, it permits the State to impose compulsory service for public purposes, including conscription and community service. **The Bonded Labour System (Abolition) Act, 1976**, has been enacted by Parliament to give effect to this Article. Article 24 prohibits the employment of children below the age of 14 years in factories, mines and other hazardous jobs. Parliament has enacted the **Child Labour (Prohibition and Regulation) Act, 1986**, providing regulations for the abolition of, and penalties for employing, child labour, as well as provisions for rehabilitation of former child labourers.

Right to Freedom of Religion: The Right to Freedom of Religion, covered in Articles 25–28, provides religious freedom to all citizens and ensures a secular state in India. According to the Constitution, there is no official State religion, and the State is required to treat all religions equally, impartially and neutrally.

Article 25 guarantees all persons the freedom of conscience and the right to preach, practice and propagate any religion of their choice. This right is, however, subject to public order, morality and health, and the power of the State to take measures for social welfare and reform. The right to propagate, however, does not include the right to convert another individual, since it would amount to an infringement of the other's right to freedom of conscience.

Article 26 guarantees all religious denominations and sects, subject to public order, morality and health, to manage their own affairs in matters of religion, set up institutions of their own for charitable or religious purposes, and own, acquire and manage a property in accordance with law.

These provisions do not derogate from the State's power to acquire property belonging to a religious denomination. The State is also empowered to regulate any economic, political or other secular activity associated with religious practice.

Article 27 guarantees that no one can be compelled to pay taxes for the promotion of any particular religion or religious institution.

Article 28 prohibits religious instruction in a wholly or partially state-funded educational institution, and educational institutions receiving aid from the State cannot compel any of their members to receive religious instruction or attend religious worship without their (or their guardian's) consent.

Cultural and Educational Rights: The Cultural and Educational rights, given in Articles 29 and 30, are measures to protect the rights of cultural, linguistic, and religious minorities, by enabling them to conserve their heritage and protecting them against discrimination.

Article 29 grants any section of citizens having a distinct language, script, or culture of its own, the right to conserve and develop the same, and thus safeguards the rights of minorities by preventing the State from imposing any external culture on them. It also prohibits discrimination against any citizen for admission into any educational institutions maintained or aided by the State, on the grounds only of religion, race, caste, language or any of them. However, this is subject to reservation of a reasonable number of seats by the State for socially and educationally backward classes, as well as reservation of up to, 50 percent of seats in any educational institution run by a minority community for citizens belonging to that community.

Article 30 confers upon all religious and linguistic minorities the right to set up and administer educational institutions of their choice in order to preserve and develop their own culture, and prohibits the State, while granting aid, from discriminating against any institution on the basis of the fact that it is administered by a religious or cultural minority. The term "minority", while not defined in the Constitution, has been interpreted by the Supreme Court to mean any community which numerically forms less than 50% of the population of the state in which it seeks to avail the right under Article 30. In order to claim the right, it is essential that the educational institution must have been established as well as administered by a religious or linguistic minority. Further, the right under **Article 30**

can be availed of even if the educational institution established does not confine itself to the teaching of the religion or language of the minority concerned, or a majority of students in that institution do not belong to such a minority. This right is subject to the power of the State to impose reasonable regulations regarding educational standards, conditions of service of employees, fee structure, and the utilization of any aid granted by it.

Right to Constitutional Remedies: Article 32 provides a guaranteed remedy, in the form of a Fundamental Right itself, for enforcement of all the other Fundamental Rights, and the Supreme Court is designated as the protector of these rights by the Constitution. The Supreme Court has been empowered to issue writs, namely ***habeas corpus, mandamus, prohibition, certiorari*** and ***quo warranto,*** for the enforcement of the Fundamental Rights, while the High Courts have been empowered under Article 226 – which is not a Fundamental Right in itself – to issue these prerogative writs even in cases not involving the violation of Fundamental Rights. The Supreme Court has the jurisdiction to enforce the Fundamental Rights even against private bodies, and in case of any violation, award compensation as well to the affected individual. Exercise of jurisdiction by the Supreme Court can also be ***suo motu*** or on the basis of a public interest litigation. This right cannot be suspended, except under the provisions of Article 226, when a state of emergency is declared.

Directive Principles of State Policy

Introduction:

The Directive Principles of State Policy can be regarded as one of the essence of the constitution. Dr. Ambedkar stated in his own words as, "Novel Feature" of the Constitution. These principles are in the way of guiding principles or recommendations to the state, they are considered the main objectives and philosophies of the union and state governments when they were making the constitution.

Meaning and Purpose of the Directive Principles of State Policy:

The Constitution of India, under Article 37 talks about the Directive Principles of State and they are present in Part IV of the Indian Constitution. Under this article it is bounded that the state has to observe these guidelines while they are making laws. These Directive Principles are reaffirmations of the principles mentioned in the Preamble of the Constitution. They are proposed to assist, as an organization to governments of the States and the Centre will act to encourage the fraternity and equality and will assure the justice and freedom to its citizens. L M Singhvi, stated about it as, "Directive Principles are the life giving provisions of the Constitution. They constitute the stuff of the Constitution and its philosophy of social justice." The Articles 36 to 51 of Part IV of the Indian Constitution deals with the Directive Principles of State Policy. They in fact gives the spiritual provision to the Fundamental Rights, this was actually carried out from the constitution of the Ireland.

Purpose: The important purpose of Directive Principles of Sate Policy is to provide social and economic justice to all its citizens and equality of opportunity and status to the people. In the Constitution of India, Article 38 talks about this as, "the State shall strive to promote the welfare of the people by securing and protecting as effectively as it may, a social order in which justice, social, economic and political shall inform all institutions of the national life. The State shall in particular minimize the inequalities in income, and endeavour to eliminate inequalities in status, facilities and opportunities, not only amongst individuals but also among groups of people residing in different areas or engaged in different vocations." If we study this principle we can understand that there is a distinction between the Directive Principles and the Fundamental Rights. The difference between Directive Principles and Fundamental Rights are stated by Gledhill, "Fundamental Rights are injunctions to prohibit the government from doing certain things, and the Directive Principles are affirmative instructions to the government to do certain things." It can also be observed that the Fundamental Rights have the legal approval and these can be enforceable in the courts whereas the Directive Principles have moral approvals and they cannot be compulsory by the courts.

The most significant part of this chapter is present in Article 39, it states that, the State shall, in particular, direct its policy towards securing:

- All the citizens must have equal means of livelihood;

- Distribution of wealth so as to subserve the common good;

- Operation of the economic system not resulting in the concentration of wealth and means of production to the common detriment;

- Equal pay for equal work for both men and women;

- Protection of adult and child labour;

 MAKING OF THE INDIAN CONSTITUTION

- Opportunities to children to develop in a healthy manner and in conditions of freedom and dignity and the protection of childhood and youth against exploitation and against moral and material abandonment;

- Provision for work and education for all people, relief in the case of unemployment, old age, sickness and disablement and in other cases of underserved want;

Article 39 says that, directing policy towards steps to equitable distribution of material resources of the community and preventing concentration of wealth in fewer hands. Article 39 (A) provide work, education and assistance in case of unemployment, old age, sickness and disablement; Article 41 says that, right to work, right to public insurance and social security.And Article 41(i) obtaining all the workers sensible wages and decent standard of life, sensible leisure and cultural opportunity;

Article 42 says that, right to humane conditions of work and maternity relief. Article 43 says that, right to a living, wage and decent standard of life, developing cottage industries (from Basu's classification - shaping the policy of the State). Article 43 (A), workers right to participate in industrial management. Article 43 (j), encourages with special care for the educational and economic interest of backwards section of the peoples such as scheduled caste and scheduled tribe. Hence, the issue of the primacy of the Directive Principles being non-justiciable over the Fundamental Rights being fully enforceable by the courts under Articles32 and 226 became a serious subject of judicial debate in the Keshavanand Bharati vs The State of Kerala case or the Fundamental Right case of 1973. While speaking on behalf of the petitioner, "When one comes to Article 31 (C) the necessity of deciding the limits of the amending powers become unmistakable. Thus Article 31 (C) violates seven essential freedoms of the constitution and makes the constitution suffer a loss of identity." The Supreme Court in accordance with its line of judicial thought as laid down in the Champakam Dorairajan case of 1951, declared clause (C) added to the Article 31 (vide 25th Constitution Amendment Act) as ultra vires of the constitution. It reiterated its stand in the Minerva Mills case of 1980. The present position, therefore, so far as the attitude of judiciary is concerned, remains the same in treating Directive Principles as subsidiary to the Fundamental Rights.

Gandhian Principles: These principle which are based on the thoughts of Gandhi:

- State must take necessary steps to systematize village panchayats and provide them with powers so that they can perform as the units of self-government; (Art 40),

- State must encourage the cottage industries of individual or in groups in rural areas; (Art 43)

- State must deliver and promote the agriculture and animal husbandry, and prevent the slaughtering of cows and other mulching animals; (Art 48)

- State must improve the public health and prohibit the intoxicating drugs and drinks; (Art 47).

To take up steps to separate judiciary from executive; to protect and preserve and maintain places of national, cultural and historical importance; To secure for all citizens a uniform civil code throughout the country; To promote international peace and security, to maintain just and honourable relations among the nations; To foster respect for international law and treaty obligations, and to encourage settlements of international disputes by arbitration.

Liberal Principles: Promotion of International Peace:

- **Article 44** directs the State to bring uniform civil code throughout the country.

- **Article 45** prescribes that the state shall provide free and compulsory education for all the children below 14 years of age. The Constitutional 86th Amendment Act 2002 stated, " The State shall endeavour to provide early childhood care and education for all children until they complete the age of six years."

- **Article 50** stipulates that the State shall take measures to separate the judiciary from the executive.

The state commands upon to make efforts according to the Article 51 of the Constitution:

- to protect international peace and its security

- to organize better relations with other nations

- to nurture respect for the international law and treaty responsibilities.

- to inspire settlements of international disputes by arbitration and with other means of peace.

 MAKING OF THE INDIAN CONSTITUTION

Directive Principles

Culture and Education:

1. The state shall attempt to provide early childhood care and education for all the children until they complete the age of 14 years (Art 45)

2. The state shall safeguard all the monuments or place or the object or historic interest and must not disfigure it. (Art 49). The other important Directive Principles are, to provide to separate the judiciary from the executive (Art 50); to obtain uniform civil code for the whole country (Art 44) and to maintain the agriculture and animal husbandry on the lines of scientific nature.

Changes to 42nd Amendment Act 1976: The new changes have been included in Part IV of the Constitution by 42nd amendment, they have inserted new Directive Principles to highlight social welfare of the constitution so that economic justice can be obtained. These are the changes they made to the constitution:

1. In the Article 39 of the clause of (f) has been inserted and it is: "that the children are given opportunities and facilities to develop in a healthy manner and in condition of freedom and dignity and that childhood and youth are protected against exploitation and against moral and material abandonment."

2. The Article 39(A) has included so that it orders the state to give "free legal aid" to all the poor and to take necessary steps to assure equal justice for all, which is present in the Preamble.

3. The Article 43 has been inserted to assure the involvement of the workers in the management of undertakings, and other industrial establishments.

4. Article 48 (A), instructs the state to safeguard and develop the environment, forest and wild life.

Sanctions of Directive Principles: These principles are not enforceable by the courts, and if the government did not satisfy the objectives then no court shall have the right to ask the government, even though they are considered as fundamental in the governance of the country and it shall be the duty of the State to apply principles while making the law (Art 37). Article 355 of the constitution says, "It shall be the duty of the Union to ensure that the Government of every State is carried on in accordance with the provisions of the Constitution." The most significant sanction behind Directive Principles is political, in the Constituent Assembly, Dr. Ambedkar observed, "if any Government ignores them, they will certainly have to answer for them before the electorates at the election time."

Importance of Directive Principles:

- **Conscience of Constitution:** The Directive Principles establish the "conscience" of the Constitution and it was stated by Justice Hegde and Justice Mukherji. The significance of it is to give definite instructions to the State to apply and implement the social and economic aspects so that there won't be any problems with non-violent social revolutions. With the help of these principles the requirements of the common people can be fulfilled and the society would improve.

- **Socialism:** In the present scenario all the states are very much preferred to have certain welfare schemes and socialism in the whole state. In the olden time the state preferred the police state but in the present situation the state is in favour of the welfare of its people. The state encourages to improve society by implementing schemes of economic, social and cultural aspects to the people. The Directive Principles protects the Constitution by providing the social political principles.

- **Diminishing the Competitive Economy:** The main objective of these principles is to diminish the consequences of competitive economy, by which it safeguards the interests of the poor. If the competition was permitted freely in the society then the effect would be directly on the poor in the society. Therefore, they promote the essence of the cooperation and common understanding in the society. By this the common person can lead a better life, irrespective of his sex, caste, creed birth, etc.

Socio-Economic Revolution by Non-Violent means:

The most significant objective which can be achieved by Directive Principles is that they promote non-violent socio-economic revolution in the society and in the country. In the present situations people are aware of the facts, and if this problem is not resolved then it would lead to revolution, hence, the exploitation of such things must be abolished. If the social justice is not provided in the state then it leads to violent struggles in the society.

Public Opinion: The significant nature of the Directive Principles is that it is the mirror image of the peoples' will and it in fact replicates

 MAKING OF THE INDIAN CONSTITUTION

by this principle. Moreover every government of the State has to give importance to Directive Principles, and they have to apply these principles when they make the law for the State. These principles are not enforced by the court still they are regarded as the most important one, because people will evaluate the performance of the political parties and their social implementations in the state by using these principles. In the true sense the sanctions behind the Directive Principles is the watchful public estimation.

Declaration of Nobel Principles: These are the principles which guides the state to provide the socio-economic aspects in the state, but these principles do not have legal force and remedies to it, but they are considered as important principles in the making of social and economic order of the state. These principles guides the state to provide the socio-economic aspects and they intensify the preamble of the constitution.

Centre - State Relations

Introduction:

The distribution of the powers is an important aspect of federalism, this constitution is rigid and flexible. The Constitution can be modified or amended and if required deleted. The Constitution is the fundamental law of the nation, and Jawaharlal Nehru stated about it as, "... The constitution cannot and should not be changed frequently. Obviously also, it can and must be changed when the situation requires it to be changed." The most important feature of the Constitution is living and improving; must be agreeable; must be rigid and flexible; and can be changeable.

Constitutional Distribution of Powers:

The relation between Centre and the States have been explained in Parts XI, XII, XIII and XVIII of the constitution in elaborate, the Part of XI is divided into two chapters and Chapter I related to the Legislative relations particularly the Articles 245 to 263 which explains about distribution of Legislative powers. The Chapter II of the Articles 256 to 263 related to Administrative Relation is divided into three parts like, General, Disputes relating to Waters, and Coordination between States. The Part XII, explains about the Finance, Property, Contracts and Suits particularly Articles of 264 to 300 deals with the above.

Legislative Relations: The Constitution of India gives a federal type of government in the country and the powers are divided among the Centre and the State. **Article 245**, gives the power to the centre to make the laws for the entire country or any portion of the country. The Constitution provides three lists such as, Union list, State list and Concurrent list, these lists can be seen in the 7th Schedule of the Constitution. The Union list contains 97 subject matters such as armed forces, defence, arms and ammunition, atomic energy, foreign affairs, diplomatic relation, United Nations treaties, citizenship, railways, shipping and navigation, telephones, airways, postal, telegraph, Reserve Bank, foreign trade, Supreme Court, Union Public Service Commission, extradition, wireless, broadcasting, foreign loans, inter-state trade and commerce, elections, etc. The parliament have some supreme powers of legislation. The State consists of 61 subjects which are mainly based on the grounds of local interest and it foresees the possibility of differentiation with regard to different items. The State legislation items consists of; public order, police, administration of justice, prisons and reformatories, local governments, public health and sanitation, intoxicating liquors, libraries, and museums, agriculture, animal husbandry, horticulture, water supplies, irrigation, land rights, fisheries, trade and commerce, gas and gas works, salaries and allowances of state officers, State Public Service Commission, roads and buildings, vehicle and taxes, etc. The state legislature has the powers to legislate. The concurrent list contains 47 subjects, in this case the subjects will be in both the centre and the state list, the concurrent list contains power, civil procedures, criminal laws, economic and social planning, marriage and divorce, education, registration of births and deaths, newspapers, books printing, legal medical and other professions, factories, foodstuff, trade unions, agriculture land, labour welfare, etc. Both the centre and state has the powers to make laws.

Article 251, states that, in case of contradiction among the laws made by the centre and state on any matter in the Union list and the law of Union will succeed.

Article 253, explains that parliament has the powers to legislate for two or more states by consent and can legislate on addition of such legislation. Article 254, says that, parliament can legislate on any matter of concurrent list and both the centre and state therefore, only parliament laws will be considered.

Article 248, confirms residuary powers of legislation on the union parliament to make laws on the concurrent list.

The Government and State List:

Sometimes the list of the centre can regulate the subjects of the state list, for instance, the parliament is given powers to assign any works to officials subordinate to governor under the Article 154(2)(b).

The parliament has powers to establish or abandon the legislative councils under the Article 169(1), if the legislature passes the resolution. If the Rajya Sabha passes a resolution with two-third majority any subject for the state list then parliament can legislate such subject according to the Article 249. In case of internal disturbances the President can impose the emergency, the parliament will have powers to make laws on the state matters. And these laws will be ineffective after six months. In case of emergency the President can authorize the parliament to exercise the powers of state legislature. Implementation of treaties, international agreements, parliament has the authority to legislate on any subject, and the law passed by the parliament cannot be invalid because it is related to the State matter. The parliament can make any other subject in the State list, the legislature of two or more States can pass resolution to give powers to make laws. By the above discussion we can understand that the Centre and State relations have importance, and Centre has the supreme powers on the States and it is higher than States and sometimes States has to entirely depend upon the Centre for certain matters.

Bills for Consideration by President:

There are some bills which requires the approval of the President after the legislation by the State Governments to enforce it. For instance, under article 31(3), law related to the property will not be valid unless it gets the approval of President, and President has the power to stay the law which he feels unreasonable. At the same time the Governor of the State has given powers under article 200 to reserve any bill for the approval of the President, and President can reject such bill and send it back to the State Government. And President is not assured to sign the same bill even though the state re-passes resolution, and there is no time limit explained for the approval of the bill.

Control over the Ordinance-making Powers of the Governor:

The Governor has the power in the state to issue the ordinance, when the state legislation is not in session, this ordinance will be passed by him after the approval from the Council of Ministers, but in some situations he can issue ordinance only with the prior approval of the President. In such cases he observes that the ordinance deals with the laws to be introduced in the legislative by the approval of the President, if the bill needs the opinion of the President so that it has to pass only after, if the law is passed by the legislature and needs the approval of President without which law is invalid, Governor looks for such three conditions before referring it to the President.

Administrative Relations between Centre and State:

The Centre has the executive powers not only on the legislation made by the parliament but has the powers to control the State as well.

Direction to the States:

Article 256, explains the respective obligation of the Centre and State Governments, "The executive powers of every state shall be so exercised as to ensure compliance with the laws made by the Parliament and any existing laws which apply in that state and the executive power of the Union shall extend to giving such direction to the state as may appear to the Government of India to be necessary for that purpose." If the State Government fails to enforce the laws of Parliament then it has the power under Article 246, it can issue direction to the State Government. The Article 257(1), says, "The executive power of every state shall be so exercised as not to impede or prejudice the exercise of the executive power of the Union, and the executive power of the Union shall extend to the giving of such directions to a state as may appear to the Government of India to be necessary for that purpose." If the state government fails to carry out any direction of the Union Government it has the power under Article 365, the President rule can be imposed.

Delegation of Union Functions to the States:

The president with the consensus of government can assign the State Government officers any action with regard to the Centre, and the States has to act as parts of the Union Government. If the state incurred extra cost then the Union Government will pay such costs.

All India Services: The services at central level such as Indian Administrative Services (IAS) Indian Police Services (IPS) , etc. the members to such services have been appointed by the President on the grounds of competitive examination conducted by the Union Public Service Commission. The parliament has the power to make new all India Services if the Rajya Sabha passes the resolution by two-third majority.

 Making Of The Indian Constitution

Inter- State Committee:

The President has the powers to make Inter -State Council among the states to bring coordination under Article 263, and it says, "If at any time it appears to the President that the public interest would be served by the establishment of a council charged with the duty of, inquiring and advising upon the disputes between the States, investigating and discussing the subject with one or more States, making suggestion upon such subject for better coordination of the policy and action with respect to the subject president can establish such council and define the nature and the duties to be performed by it and its organizations."

Full Faith and Credit to Public Acts:

The Parliament has the powers to make laws of public acts and the final orders/judgments or passed by civil courts in any part of India are executable anywhere within India in accordance with law.

Inter-State Water Dispute:

The Parliament has the powers to make laws regarding the inter-state dispute over the river or river valley water by the constitution. The Parliament has authority to exclude such disputes from the jurisdiction of the courts, including the Supreme Court.

Telangana centre has formed water boards to look after the disputes arising between the states of Andhra Pradesh and Telangana. During emergency President has the powers to give orders to the State Governments. The Parliament can establish a commission on the inter-state commerce and trade activities.

Financial Relations:

It is to be understood that the financial resources of the Centre and State must be adequate so that they can discharge their respective accountabilities under the constitution. The financial commission allocates, adjusts and receives finance from certain sources. The Constitution of India provides the scheme for the distribution of the revenue resources among the Centre and the State governments.

It is divided in two parts

1. The allocations of revenue between the union and states and
2. The distribution of grant-in-aid.

According to this there are different sources of revenue for the Union Government and State Government. There are certain taxes which are levied and collected by the Union Government but assigned to the States at the same time the State Government collects the tax on behalf of the Union Governments. Under the Article, 269, taxes are collected by Central Government on behalf of the State Government. They are as follows:

1. Duties in respect of succession to property other than agricultural land,

2. Estate duty other than agriculture land,

3. Taxes on railway fares and freights,

4. Taxes other than stamp duties, advertisements and published therein,

5. Terminal taxes on goods or passengers by railways, sea and air,

6. Taxes from the sale or purchase of newspapers,

7. The taxes other than newspapers or inter-state trade or commerce.

Under **Article 268**, of the Constitution the State Government collects and assigns to Union Government such as, stamp duties, excise on medicinal and toilets preparation (those shall be mentioned in the Union list) shall be levied by the Government of India but shall be collected, in the case where such duties are leviable within any Union Territory, by the Government of India, and in other cases, by the States within which such duties are respectively leviable. There are certain taxes which are collected by the Union Government but it will distribute those taxes to the State Governments under Article 270 and 272.

Finance Commission:

Article 280 provides for the establishment of a Financial Commission. Every five years, the President has the authority to appoint the Finance Commission. The commission actually suggests regarding the allocation of revenues to the centre and state governments, and grants-in-aid to other states and financial institutions. The President has to place all the recommendation of the commission along with explanatory memorandum to both the houses of parliaments.

Audit-General of India:

The Comptroller and Audit General of India is accountable for the maintenance and audit of the Union and State Governments and is the official of the Central Government. He is appointed by the President. But his powers and duties are determined by the Parliament. The forms for the maintenance of accounts are arranged by the Comptroller and Audit General (CAG) and has no say in the matter by the States.

Actual Operation of the Centre-State Relations:

It will be better to have good relations between the Centre and the State Governments, every effort has been made to strengthen such relations where the centre is already stronger than the states. C. Rajagopalachari remarked that, "The independence of the States is being forgotten and a unitary state is being established in India thoughtlessly."

The Third Amendment Act made to alter item 33 of the concurrent list in 1954, increased the authority of Union Government over the production, distribution and prices of many commodities. With the Sixth Amendment Act inserted new item 9-A to the Union list in 1956, thereby reduced the powers of the state legislature with regard to imposition of sales tax by states. With the Seventh Amendment Act inserted section 350-A to the constitution in 1956, by giving special powers to Centre to give primary education to the linguistic minority groups in their own language.

North-Eastern Council (NEC): These zones are mainly established to carry out the programmes of centre, these councils deliberated the means of implementing the policy of the union such as, food, conservation, saving and water conservation. The region of north-eastern has unusual problem, it consisted of seven states such as, Arunachal Pradesh, Assam, Manipur, Meghalaya, Mizoram, Nagaland and Tripura. The region has tactical significance because it has common boundaries with diverse nations such as, Burma, Bangladesh, China and Bhutan, and it is connected to India by a small strip of land. It was set up under the NEC Act of 1971, this act was passed in the parliament in December 1971. The Council contains the Governor and Chief Minister of the seven states. President can nominate Union Minister to this Council. The important function of this is to make balance of the socio-economic improvements in the region by the coordinated original planning. The Council will develop the infrastructure in the region and increase economic improvement in the region by starting power, industrial, agricultural, flood control and communication projects. It must be noted that it is an advisory body and it has no powers to raise the financial resources.

Inter-State Council:

Under Article 263, by the recommendations made by the Sarkaria Commission, the Government of India established inter-state council in May

1990. It contains the Prime Minister as the Chairman, Chief Ministers of all States, Administrators of the Union Territories without legislature and Prime Minister nominates six Union Cabinet Ministers as its members. It is only a recommendatory body and its main functions are investigating and discussing such subject of states of common interest, making recommendations for better coordination of policy and action, discussing such matter with the chairman.

Control Boards:

This board looks after the problems of the water distribution and it was inserted as Article 262(1) in the constitution. It provides the parliament to "provide for adjudication of any dispute or complaint with respect to the use, distribution or control of the water of, or in, any Inter-State river or river valley." There are many rivers which originate in some place and run in India, there are rivers like Kaveri, flowing through a number of states, same case with Godavari and Krishna they also flow in different states like Maharashtra, Karnataka and now Telangana and finally into Andhra Pradesh. To solve the problem with the states it constituted a Corporation, the **Damodar Valley Corporation** for the states of Bihar and West Bengal. They have made control boards to solve this problem. There are 14 boards at present, the **Kosi Control Board** and **Nagarjuna Control Board** are examples of that. The Control Board has a Governor, Chief Minister and Central Minister in this board. Their functions are approval of design of the project and to monitor and review progress, to mention contracts view the costs, to make arrangements to rehabilitate persons displaced in project works.

Regional Electricity Boards:

The other important requirement in inter-state cooperation is the making of electricity grids. Since independence, throughout the country we had severe power crisis. To overcome this problem of electricity these grids came into existence. The Government made a policy on electricity with certain aims of assuring proper supply at minimum cost, for this an autonomous body called as **Energy Management Centre**, was established in 1989 as a nodal agency. In order to supply the power the nation has been divided into five zones, like North, East, North-East West, and South zones. These boards are advisory in function; they review the progress of power development methods in the region; they plan and guarantee integrated operations of all power systems in the region; makes the maintenance programme; operation schedule will be prepared; determine the amount of surplus power for the exchange between the States; determine the tariff structure; etc.

Recommendations of Sarkaria Commission on Centre-State Relations:

The Constitution of India provided the two-tier government, one at the centre and other at the different states. There are problems between the relation of the Centre and States, working of such system there is a danger for the unity and integrity of the nation. There is a need to have consensus and cooperation among them. To sort out this problem in March 1983, the then Prime Minister Indira Gandhi, announced the proposal to appoint the commission. R.S Sarkaria, a retired Judge of the Supreme Court was the Chairman of the Commission. She said that, "the commission would review the existing arrangements between the Centre and States while keeping in view the social and economic developments that have taken place over the years. The review will take into account the importance of unity and integrity of the country for promoting the welfare of the people." She also pronounced that Commission would test "the working of the existing arrangements between the Centre and the States and recommend such changes in the said arrangements as might be appropriate within the present constitutional framework."

The Commission was established according to the Government of India, Ministry Of Home Affairs, notification **No: IV/11017/1/83-CSR,** dated 9th June 1983.

Important Recommendations of the Commission: The report of the Commission was submitted and published in 1988, it had two parts, and the first part is about the report and the second part are the memorandums received from the different State governments and political parties. The report covered, inter-governmental relations upon the legislative and administration areas and also reported the requirement for establishing a Standing Inter-State Council under Article 263, to give more assurance to Inter-State coordination.

Which includes - Emergency provisions, Governor's Role, Deployment of Union's Armed Forces in the State to sort out the problem of public order, Reservation of the State Bills for the attention of President and All India Services. The report also studied the relation between the inter-governmental relations such as, social-economic development, financial relations, economic and social planning, national economic and development council. The items such as, agriculture, issues related to industries, mines, and minerals, inter-sate trade and commerce, river disputes, food and civil supplies, forests and mass media. It also studied the matters related to language, Union Territories, and general observation and conclusions.

The Recommendations: With regard to legislative relations, the residuary powers of legislation which related to taxation must be in the concurrent list and constitution has to be amended accordingly. A resume of the views of the State government and the comments of the inter-state council must go with the Bill while introduced in the Parliament. With regard to administrative relations, there are some arguments present regarding the Centre-State relations, they have very severe complaints about the Articles 256, 257 and 365. The 256, article says that, the executive powers of every state shall be so exercised so as to ensure compliance with the laws made by Parliament.

While Article 257, says that, the executive powers of every State shall be so exercised as not to impede or prejudice the exercise of the executive power of the Union, shall extend to giving of such directions to a State as may appear to the Government of India to be necessary for the purpose. And Article 365, states that, if a State fails to comply with or give effect to, any directions given by the Union Government, it shall be lawful for the President to hold that a situation has risen in which the Government of State cannot be carried on in accordance with the provisions of the Constitution. The Commission also views the authority of Parliament foreseen in the Articles 246 and 254 is essential and there is no need to change them, the only suggestion given in this regard is that the residual matters other than taxation must be included in the concurrent list

The Indian Parliament

Introduction:

The Parliament of India contains the President, Prime Minister, Lok Sabha and the Rajya Sabha. The Lok Sabha and Rajya Sabha are otherwise known as the two Houses, Upper House and Lower House. The Upper House or Rajya Sabha is called Council of States while the Lower House is called House of the People or Lok Sabha. President is not from either of houses hence, he will not attend the Parliament, but he addresses both the Houses. In fact the Article 79 of Chapter 2 controlled in Part V in the Constitution titled "Union" provides the Union Legislature. The Indian Parliament is always compared with the British Parliament, but if we observe the reality is that there is total difference between them particularly about the scope of powers. The Parliament of British is a sovereign legislature and Indian Parliament is not as strong as British, the powers of Indian Parliament are very restricted due to the checks by the Constitution and the Fundamental Rights assured to the people of India. The Acts passed by the British cannot be challenged in any court but it can be challenged in India.

Composition/Term and Qualification of Members:

Rajya Sabha/Council of States:

The Parliament of India is bicameral while the Rajya Sabah is Upper House and the representatives from the different States forms this house. Under the Article 80 of the Constitution the Council of States shall consist of not more than 250 members, of whom 12 shall be nominated by the President and the remaining 238 shall be from the representatives of the States and Union Territories. The persons who were appointed by President will be from different fields like persons from literature, science, arts, and social service.

Whereas the representatives of the States will be elected by elected members of the Legislative Assemblies of the States, according to the proportional representation. In case the representatives are from Union Territories, the law will be made by the Parliament. Under this the representatives shall be elected indirectly by the members of an electoral college for that territory, according to the proportional representative system of single transferable vote.

Qualifications:

To be elected to the Upper House, a person must be a citizen of India, must have 30 years of age, and must be a parliamentary elector in the concerned State from where he pursues election. A person may be disqualified if he must not hold any public office either in Centre or State or must not hold any Ministerial position; or must not be of unsound mind; or un-discharged unsolved insolvent; if disqualified by or under any law made by Parliament.

Term:

The Council of States is a permanent body and it cannot be dissolved, the term of each member will be for six years and one-third of its members will retire every second year. The Vice-President of the nation is the ex-officio Chairman of the Council of States. The members of the council will elect from them the Deputy Chairman.

Chairman of the Rajya Sabha:

As per Article 89 of the Indian Constitution, the Vice-President of India acts as the chairman of the Rajya Sabha. The chairman is not a member of the House. The members of the Parliament elect him for every five years not as the chairman of the Rajya Sabha but as the Vice-President of India. It implies that both the members of the Lok Sabha and the Rajya Sabha cast their vote in the Vice-Presidential elections. The Vice-President receives his salary in the capacity of the chairman of the Rajya Sabha. At present he is paid Rs. 1,40,000/- towards monthly salary. Besides, he is entitled to other allowances, office, boarding and travelling facilities. His salaries and allowances are charged on the Consolidated Fund of India.

Powers and Functions of the Rajya Sabha:

The Rajya Sabha has Legislative, Financial, Electoral, powers to remove the President and other officers.

The power of the Upper House is as equal as the Lower House while in such cases of ordinary legislation. Bill can be originated in any of the House. A bill cannot be said to pass unless both the houses have agreed to it, either by amendment or without it. In the case of deadlocks both the Houses will have a joint session by the President. Any Bill may be passed or rejected in either of the houses or may be rejected in both the Houses and hence, needs amendments in the bill. If more than six months has passed from the date of receipt without passing of the bill then President will call for the joint session of the Houses and in that session if the bill is passed with majority by the members from both Houses present at the time of voting then it will be deemed to have been passed by the both Houses

Financial Powers:

With regard to the financial aspect the Upper House does not have any powers, the bill of Finance is not supposed to enter in this house, only the finance bill which is passed in the Lok Sabha will be sent for the suggestion of the Upper House. The Upper House must return such bill within 14 days of time with their recommendation, in case if it is not returned within the stipulated time frame of 14 days then it will be deemed as the bill has been passed in both the Houses. If the Upper House returns the Bill for amendments to the Lower House then the Lower House considers it and thereafter it is deemed to have the bill passed in both the Houses.

     MAKING OF THE INDIAN CONSTITUTION

Powers to remove President and other officers:

If the President of India violates the Constitution, in such cases, the Constitution has the provision to remove the President from the office by impeachment, the charge can be made by either of the house. If the Council of States makes the charge against him then the Lower House will examine it vice versa. While the agency which examines and passes the resolution by a majority of two-thirds of the total number of members of the House that the charge has been sustained, the President is removed. The Council of States can remove the Vice-President from the office by a resolution passed by a majority of all the members present in the council and accepted by the Lower House or the House of the People. Further, a Judge of a Supreme Court or High Court can be removed from the office by an order of the President after he addresses in both houses and supported by majority of the house not less than two-thirds of members of the house and voting has been presented to the President, and the same way the Auditor-General of India would be removed.

Control over the Executive:

Article 75 of the Constitution says that, Council of Ministers shall be collectively responsible to House of the People and some of the Ministers will be chosen from the Upper House. The Council has control over the Union Executive by pursuing information by way of questions and supplementary and by way of moving adjournments, but it cannot toss out the Council of Ministers.

Constituent Functions:

The Upper House as well has the similar sort of powers like Lower House to amend the Constitution. Under article 368, amendment can be introduced in any of the Houses once this is introduced. It has to be passed by a majority of two-third of the total members of that house in voting. The constitution did not deliberate any procedure for settling variances in the disparity on the issue of amendment.

Electoral Powers:

The members of the house has the power to participate in the election of the President and the Vice President, They are the members of the Electoral College.

Miscellaneous Functions:

The Upper House would pronounce by a resolution which has the support of two-thirds majority that it is very much required in the interest of the country must make laws related to any sort which included in the State list specified in the particular resolution. They can also by passing resolution can say to Parliament to create one or more All India Services to the Union and States and organize the recruitment and other such activities.

Criticism:

It is evident that the House of the States is not as strong as the Lower House in making decisions. It is due to the fact that it is unable to have control over the executive. Another reason is that the Council does not have powers on the financial matters, but at the same time it does not match its powers in this regard but otherwise it is equivalent to Lower House in other matters. A part from this has certain powers which the Lower House does not have, it can declare that in the interest of the nation parliament must make laws on the subject included in the State list and can recommend making of new All India services.

Lok Sabha/Lower House:

Article 81, provided the composition of the Lok Sabha. The maximum number consist of 552 members and out of which 20 members are elected by the specified process of Parliament for the representation of the Union Territories and not more than 2 members from Anglo-Indian community. Out of these members 530 are directly elected to the Parliament by the people. According to Article 81(2), the number of representatives from each state by the way of ratio between that the number of the population of the State is, so far as practicable, the same for all the States.

Term and Qualification of Lok Sabha Members:

Qualification:

To be elected to the Lower House, a person must be a citizen of India, must be 25 years of age, and must be a parliamentary elector in the concerned state from where he pursues election. He must have such other qualifications as prescribed by the Parliament. A person may be disqualified if he must not hold any public office either in Centre or State or must not hold any Ministerial position; or must not be of unsound mind; or insolvent; if disqualified by or under any law made by Parliament.

By the Representation of People's Act laid down some other qualification; A person must not have been found guilty by a Court or an Election Tribunal of certain election offences or by the way of corrupt practices in the election; he must not have been convicted by the court

    MAKING OF THE INDIAN CONSTITUTION

of offence and sentenced to imprisonment for a period not less than two years; he must not have failed to lodge account for his election within the time; He must not have dismissed from the Government service on the charges of corruption or not loyal to the State government; he must not hold any office of profit or any corporation in which Government has financial interest; He must not have any interest in the contracts of the Governments, any execution of such works.

Term of the House:

The Lower House will last for a period of five years from the date of its existence in the House, but it can be dissolved by the President where it undergoes the no-confidence motion and motion passed or in case of emergency till the revoke of emergency.

Speaker of the House:

Article 93 to 97 of Indian constitution deals with the office of the Speaker of the Lok Sabha. The Speaker of the House is the presiding officer of the house. The House elects the Speaker from the members of the Lok Sabha. The Speaker is always elected from the majority party of the house. The Speaker will be in the office till the life of the House or till he resigns from the office. Speaker will be in the office even if the House is dissolved, till the first meeting of the newly elected House. The framers of the Constitution wanted that the Speaker of Lok Sabha must be non-partisan person like that of Speaker of the British House of the Commons, but in reality the Speaker of Lok Sabha is not as impartial as the Speaker of House of the Commons, because here the Speaker is the member of the party. Though the Speaker does not take active role in the discussions but it is understood that he/she has the reservations for the party. At present Speaker receives a monthly salary of Rs.1,40,000/-. Besides, he is provided with rent free residential, medical, travelling and communication facilities. His salaries and allowances are charged on the Consolidated Fund of India. The Speaker may be removed if the Speaker loses his post or if he loses the membership in the house or by resignation submitted to the post. The Speaker may be removed from the office by the passing of resolution of the house with majority of the then members of the House. In such case, 14 days prior notice has to be served before the resolution. When such a resolution is in process Speaker cannot preside, but he has the right to speak.

Deputy Speaker:

As per article 93 of our Constitution, there will be a Deputy Speaker in the Lok Sabha along with the Speaker. This office was created for conducting the meetings of the Lok Sabha in the absence of the Speaker. The Deputy Speaker, like the speaker, is elected by the members of the Lok Sabha from among themselves. Like the Speaker, the Deputy Speaker may be removed from his office. The Deputy Speaker, while acting as the presiding officer, enjoys all the powers and privileges of the speaker. Another point to be noted is that if the Deputy Speaker is a member of one of the parliamentary committees, he will act as the chairman of that committee. He is authorized to participate in the meetings of various committees connected to the Lok Sabha. He has freedom to participate in the meetings of the Lok Sabha like other members on all other occasions. He can express his views on bills, cast his vote on bills and continue his relations with the party.

Powers and Functions of the Lok Sabha:

Legislative Powers: The powers of the Lok Sabha is supreme, it has the same powers like the Upper House but the supreme powers lies in financial matters. It has the final go in respect of such bill. No bill can become law unless it is passed in both the Houses of the Parliament. The President can preside only on occasions of disagreement between the Houses and issues can be settled by the members by voting who are present. A joint session can be addressed by the President only if six months has elapsed from the date of receipt of the bill in the House and bill is not passed by the House.

Financial Powers: With regard to the matters of the finance the power of the Lok Sabha is final and supreme.A bill related to money has to be introduced in the Lok Sabha and the bill passed by the Lok Sabha will be sent to the Rajya Sabha for its recommendations. The State Council must have to send back the Bill within 14 days of time with their suggestions, the Lower House may agree or may agree some of it or it can totally reject their recommendation. If the Upper House in case does not send in prescribed time then it is deemed that the Bill is passed in both the Houses of the Parliament.

Making and Control over Council of Ministers:

It is evident that the House of the People can make the Council of Ministers, the leader of the largest party and who is appointed by the President is known as the Prime Minister. The Ministers may be from either of the houses. The Minister's Council is accountable to the Lok Sabha, it can remain in the office till it has the confidence of the house. The representatives of the Lok Sabha have the control of administration by way of questions, supplementaries, adjournment motions and censure

 ⚒ MAKING OF THE INDIAN CONSTITUTION

motions. It can remove the Ministers by passing a vote of No-confidence motion.

Constituent Powers: The Lower House has similar sort of powers like Upper House to amend the Constitution. Under article 368, amendment can be introduced in any of the Houses. Once this is introduced it has to be passed by a majority of two third of the total members of that house in voting.

Committees of the Lok Sabha:

Indian Parliament has different committees. It is not conceivable to all the members to understand the details and technicalities present in the legislative measures, hence the work of Parliament is mostly done by the Committees.

There are three committees. They are:

1. Those which are mostly apprehensive with organiZation of powers of the House,

2. Support the House in their legislative functions; and

3. Committees which deals with financial matters and scrutinize the activities of the Government.

In the first category, we can see committees such as, Business Advisory Committee, The Rules Committee, The Committee on the Privileges and the Committee on Absence of the Member.

In the second category, Select Committee, Joint Select Committee, Committee on the Private Member's Bills and Resolutions, Committee on the Subordinate Legislation.

The function of the **Rules Committee** is that, to consider matters of procedure and conduct business in the House and suggest required changes in them. The role of **Business Committee** is to guarantee smooth working of the committee, on its advice Speaker organizes the Business of the House. The main function of the **Committee on Privileges** is to safeguard the privileges, if it violates it refers it to the committee. The function of the **Select Committee** on Bills has the powers to examine the witness, collect information and take expert advice. The role of **General Purpose Committee** is it considers proposals and advices the Speaker in matters related to organization and development of the House. The **Committee on Private Members Bills and Resolutions** examines the bills of the Private members.

The function of the Committee on Subordinate Legislation has the power to frame rules and regulations, and are known as **Subordinate Legislation** or Delegated Legislation. The role of **Public Accounts Committee** is to examine the reports of the Comptroller and Audit General of India and check the accounts of the Government related to financial transactions. The function of the Committee and the Government Assurances is to scrutinize the assurances, promises, undertakings, etc. given by Ministers on the floor and to report on the extent to which they have been implemented, etc. The function of the Committee on Petitions is to examine petitions submitted to the house by individuals or organizations which are to address their grievances.

Legislative Procedures: There are two types of Bills, **Ordinary Bills and Money Bills.** The Ordinary Bills may be divided further into two classes, they are **Government Bills** and **Private Members Bills.** All the Bills except Money Bills and Financial Bills may be introduced in either of the house but Money Bill can be introduced in the Lok Sabha only. In the first instance, the Bill will be prepared by the concerned ministry and it works out all the implications such as political, financial and administrative aspects. The Attorney-General of India and Ministry of Law will be consulted to check the legalities and constitutional problems. After that ministry prepares memorandum for the Cabinet, then the Cabinet may approve or may refer to Standing Committee. After the approval of the Cabinet the sponsoring ministry sends it to the Draftsmen with all related papers, after the preparation of the Draft, ministry examines it and then the Bill is ready for introduction in the house. The concerned minister gives a notice of motion to introduce the Bill. On the day appointed for the introduction of the Bill the Speaker or the Chairman calls the minister who moves the motion for leave to introduce the Bill. No debates takes place at this stage, if the bill is opposed by any member then the minister and the opponents are given a chance to explain their views. If there is opposition on constitutional grounds, speaker may permit a full debate in which the Attorney-General would involve. The speaker puts to the house questions, it wants the Bill to be considered for passage, if the majority members support it then the bill is deemed to have been moved, otherwise it is lost. If the first reading of the Bill is over then it is published in the Gazette of India. The second reading of the Bill is divided into two phases, the mover of the Bill may make one of the three motions such as,

1. Bill be referred to a Select Committee,

 MAKING OF THE INDIAN CONSTITUTION

2. Circulated for eliciting public opinion;

3. Be taken for consideration by the House immediately.

Generally first two cases they choose, if Bill is moved under immediate consideration any other member of the House may move an amendment proposing one of the two other options. If the motion of circulation of the Bill is carried then the Bill is published in the State Gazette, and opinions of the public are invited. The opinions received from the public are circulated, then the stage for the second reading comes the Bill moves the motion referred to Select or Joint Committees, the motion have a debate and no amendments are accepted at this stage. The next stage is Committee stage, if the House chooses to the Committee then the member from the house will be nominated by the Speaker as Chairman and it will study in depth about the measures and provisions. They examine the Bill clause wise and they recommend for amendments and if they have the differences then the report is made by the majority of the members. Next stage is the Report Stage when Committee examines it thoroughly, then the Chairman of the Committee present the Report to the House. House goes clause wise about the Bill and it is free to move amendments, when the clauses have been discussed the Bill is said to cross the report stage and listed for the third reading. In the third reading the Bill is presented in the House, at this stage no considerable alterations are made, Lastly, the Bill is put to vote and if it is passed by the majority of the members present and voting, it is declared by the Speaker. Then the Bill will be send to the other house to pass if it is passed by the other House as well then it is sent to the President for the approval. When the Bill is passed in both the Houses it reaches the President for the approval President either can approve or withhold the approval. If it rejects the bill it will be sent back to the House for reconsideration, House reconsiders it accordingly then sends it to the President for approval, President cannot withhold therefrom.

Passing of the Budget:

Budget is the annual financial statement of the Government, it is provided in the Article 112 that the President shall in respect of every financial year cause to be laid before both Houses of Parliament. The Budget is prepared by the Ministry of Finance and Finance Minister will read the budget in the Lok Sabha. The Budget is the Income and Expenditure statements of the year.

General Debate on the Budget: The Minister of Finance presents the Budget in the Lok Sabha with a speech in which he gives the financial position of the country, frameworks of economic and fiscal policy of the government, and gives a chance to every member to evaluate the entire administration and their grievances.

Voting of Demands for Grants: After completion of the general discussions on the budget is finished, the Upper House has no role in it, the voting of grants and demands for expenditure made by the Government is the elite business of the Lower House. Each Ministry demand their grants which are accessible distinctly and voted. Every demand will be in the form of motion, and a time limit of one month will be given.

Appropriation Bill: Later the grants which have been allotted by the Lower House, a Bill will be put in the House for appropriation out of the Consolidated Funds of India. The amount must not be beyond the amount stated in their statement before the Parliament. This Bill will be presented in the Lok Sabha but there will not be any amendments to such Bill.

Finance Bill: After the Bill of Appropriation is passed the disposal of the expenditure makes the completion of the Budget. They also levy taxes and a separate bill of Finance Bill is made and introduced in the Lok Sabha which has the proposals of the revenue. The Finance Bill goes through the similar procedure as the Money Bill.

Control on the Powers of the Indian Parliament: There are limitations on the power of the Parliament, the constitution is written and it has the definite restrictions on its powers. It has been clearly mentioned in the Constitution about the powers of Parliament along with other organizations and their authority. It does not have full authority in making of the law like Britain, and it cannot amend all the provisions of the Constitution. Only some of them can be amended. It is due to the fact that the Federal structure of the Constitution has some restrictions to it, the Federal type of polity is another reason. The powers have been divided among the Union and State Governments both will get those authority from the Constitution. There are three lists such as, **Union List, State List and Concurrent list.** Parliament has the right to legislate on the subjects of Union List whereas the States are empowered to make laws on the State List, but at any situation Parliament can legislate State List. Parliament cannot amend the Constitution so as to alter its primary feature . It cannot amend the Constitution unless it has the support of half of the States.

The Fundamental Rights are also one of the restriction on the authority of the Parliament. Article 13(1) stated that all the laws will be applicable as soon as the Constitution emerges, they are not consistent of the Provisions of Part III that deals with the Fundamental Rights. In case all the provisions of 42nd Constitution Amendment Act were permitted to stand then all the powers would have been with the Parliament and it would have taken all the Fundamental Rights of citizens. The other reason for the limitation of powers is judicial review, it is under the watch of the judiciary, Supreme Court has authority to reject any legislative enactment as unconstitutional. Therefore, it is a wrong notion that Parliament is sovereign body.

Decline of Indian Parliament:

Legislative Power: There are four kinds of authorities as given to Parliament. They are legislative, financial, administrative and constitutional powers. It is understandable that the Parliament will make laws on all the subjects related to Union and Concurrent list, but in reality the whole process will be under the control of the Prime Minister, and most of the Bill will be introduced by the Council of Ministers. A private member Bill will not be accepted except it has the backing of Government. If the Parliament has to pass the Bill then Government would not support it, on most of the situations Government overlooks the Parliament's law making authority by enacting legislation by ordinances.

Financial Powers: It has the supreme authority. No tax can be increased and no expenditure can be incurred without the Parliament's advice. But the fact is that the entire show is run by the Cabinet, Parliament does its duties in an obligatory way. It has to submit the demands for grants through Consolidated Fund of India. Parliament cannot demand any grants except on the recommendation of the President.

Constituent Powers: The other significant authority is to amend the Constitution. In this case also the initiation lies with the Government. The amendments which are introduced by the Government only would be passed and the Bills introduced by the private member will be rejected.

Administrative Powers: The Article 75 states that the Council of Ministers are collectivly accountable to the Lok Sabha, which means that as long as the Ministers remains in the office and Parliament becomes unsuccessful because Prime Minister has the power to dissolve the parliament at any given time. In the year 1970, the then Prime Minister Indira Gandhi advised the President to dissolve the Parliament and same case happened with Morarji Desai. he too advised the President in 1979.

Reason of Decline of Parliament: There are several reasons for this decline, firstly, there is one party dominance throughout the years except for a brief period like in 1969-70 because of split in Congress then in 1977-79, Janta rule, but in 1980 again Congress emerged victorious.

Rigid Party Discipline: Only the Congress party was able to maintain the control over the parliamentary wing and the 52nd Amendment Act of 1985 further strengthened its control over the party. Whereas other parties had no control over the party, most of the parties which were contested along with Congress have now vanished. The other important factor for the discipline was that the party members in the parliament would be under the control of the Prime Minister this was another advantage to the Congress party to have such control over them.

Weak Opposition: The most important factor for this was due to the weak opposition in the Parliament, the attempt to make a strong opposition were unsuccessful till date. The other significant reason for the decline was due to the delegated legislation. It is a fact that Parliament has no time to look after all its duties and the experienced administrators tackles the problems.

President of India

Introduction:

The power in a democratic way lies with the people, the administration is the executive organization for the implementation of the government policies and programmes which are accepted by the Parliament. The Constitution of India under the Article 52, says that there shall be a President of India, and President is the head of the country and according to the article 53, all the executive powers are with the President only. The expression of "executive power" is not defined in the Constitution. All the others are directly or indirectly subordinate to the President. All the executive activities are done under the Presidents' name.

Qualification to be a President of India:

The qualifications to be the President of India:

1. Must be a citizen of India;

2. Must have completed 35 years of age;

3. Must be qualified as a member of the House of People which means (must be registered as a voter in any Parliamentary constituency);

4. Must not hold any office of profit under Government of India, or under any State Government or under local authority which are directly or indirectly related to the Government's control;

The Article 58, further says that, person shall not be deemed to hold any office or profit; and hence qualified for being a candidate for Presidentship. They are the President, Vice President, and Governor of the State, the Minister of Union or the State. There are certain conditions, according to the Article 59, President cannot be a member of the Parliament or Legislature of any State, if held, then elected President shall be deemed to have vacated seat in that office on the date on which he enters upon his office as President. The President shall not hold any other office of profit.

Term in the Office:

Generally, President will be in the office for five years, unless President is removed by the Parliament by impeachment for violating the Constitution of India. The President gets a salary of Rs 1, 50,000 P M and allowances. Salary and allowances cannot be reduced during the term of office.

Election of the President:

The Article 54, says that President shall be elected by an electoral college, hence, the election of the President is not direct which means people of India will not take part in the election.

The Electoral College contains of

1. The elected members of the Lok Sabha and Rajya Sabha;

2. The elected members of the Legislative Assemblies of the States. The 70th Amendment of 1992, inserted in the Article 54, which provides the word "state' includes the National Capital Territory of Delhi, Union Territory of Pondicherry, the MLAs from these areas are included to the Electoral College. Article 62, says that, mandatory time limit and the election cannot be postponed beyond the expiration of the President's tenure.

3. Every legislature of the State will have as much votes as there are of 1000 in the quotient attained by dividing the number of population of the State by the total number of elected members of the Assembly, this is known as the "Weightage" determined by the population of

each state. The states with more population such as Uttar Pradesh, Bihar, etc., will have larger number of votes than the states where the population is comparatively lesser. There should be equality among the States and the Union, which means the Member of Parliament will have same number of votes as the total of the votes of the elected representatives to the State Assemblies. The election will have the system of proportional representation i.e.

The person who gets absolute majority will be declared elected as the President of India. The election of the President is not direct hence, it is indirect by which the Electoral College will elect the President of India. It is significant to note that the nominated members to both Houses of Parliament and the States will not have the right to vote in the election process of the President. The process of the election of the President is mainly grounded on the proportional representation which means a single transferable vote system. In this election they follow the secret ballot only. To get consistency in the representation of the States and for the equality between the Centre and the States they follow an exclusive process to bring the estimation of the number of votes to be cast by each member. To achieve this the total population of every State will be divided by the number of legislatures of the State. The quotient or figure attained is then divided by 1000. This gives the number of votes to be cast by each elected member of Assembly of the particular state. In case the reminder surpasses 500, then the number of votes is increased by one.

The Powers of the President:

The President of India will be in office for the period of five years, he/she will have the identity of the nation, President enjoys number of privileges and immunities which are not amenable to the jurisdiction of any law court in the country, cannot be arrested or imprisoned. No one can ask the authority of the President. The President will have distinct powers such as, executive, legislative, financial, military, judicial and emergency powers.

Executive Powers: The Constitution has provided the executive powers to the President under the Article 77, and exercises by the help of Council of Ministers. All the activities of the government will be done under the name of the President of India. At the same time President has the powers to appoint any one to the office and can remove from the office. The President appoints the Prime Minister and on the advice the other Council of Ministers, Governors, Chief Justice, Election Commissioners, Judges to the Supreme Court and High Court, Chairman and Members of the Union

     MAKING OF THE INDIAN CONSTITUTION

Public Service Commission (UPSC), etc. President has the authority to nominate 12 members to the Rajya Sabah as well, can also appoint inter-state council and ask for the advice in case of any dispute between the states. President will appoint the ambassadors to different countries and at the same time will receive ambassadors from other counties, can declare war and can negotiate peace talks with the countries, has the power and authority over the state governments, has the authority to know about the developments in the country and affairs of the Governments. The Union territories will administer in the name of the President, and has the authority to ask the Union Council of Ministers about any decision they take.

Legislative Powers: The President of India is the constituent part of the Union Parliament, President has the authority to summon and prorogue both Houses of Parliament and can dissolve them as well. But the Article 85(1), forces limitation on this authority. The President has the power to summon the parliament within six months form the last sitting, if at all any disagreement among the members of the two houses then President can call a joint session according to Article 108, in the joint session he gives the speech about the performance of the government, the speech would be similar to that of the King in England, may send the message to both the Houses according to the Article 86. Each Bill which passes in both Houses will be sent to the President for the approval according to the Article 111, may give assent or withhold the Bill, may send it back to the House from where it came for reconsideration, but it does not apply to the money bill. All the Bills before it is introduction has to get the assent of the President, the Bill for the formation of new states, the approval is very much necessary.

Ordinance-making Authority: The President of India has the authority to make ordinance according to the Article 123, of the Constitution, it is the most important legislative powers of the President. Any time when both Houses are in session then if feels it is necessary to take action in the interest of the nation the President can issue ordinance according to the circumstances of that point of time. The issued ordinance will have similar force like that of Parliament Act. Even Court cannot enquire into the reasons for it.

Financial Powers: The President of India has some of the financial powers as well. The annual budget of the country which is presented by the Finance Minister in the Parliament will be on behalf of the President.

Without the approval of the President no money bill like proposal for rising the taxation, demands for grants cannot be introduced in the Parliament. President has the authority over the Contingency Fund of India. President has the authority to appoint the Financial Commission to make suggestions on the financial matters between Centre and the States.

Judicial Powers: The Judges of Supreme Court and the High Court are appointed by the President of India. ,The President has to be consulted before making rule and procedures for the Supreme Court. The President has the authority of pardoning. Under the Article 72 of the Constitution to grant pardon, reprieves, respites or remission of punishment or to suspend, remit or commute the sentence of any person convicted of any offence such as, by Court Martial; an offence against any law relating to the matter to which executive power of the Union extends; or in all cases in which death sentence has been awarded.

Military Powers: The President is the Supreme Commander of the Armed Forces, it has the authority to declare wars, conclude treaties or make peace on behalf of the nation. These powers by the President is "regulated by law", but the authority of the military by the President can be regulated by the Parliament, without the emission of the Parliament he cannot declare war nor he can have peace treaties.

Diplomatic Powers: The head of the State has the powers to receive the ambassadors from different countries and other diplomatic persons, can send such persons to other nations on his behalf. All the treaties and negotiations and international agreements done on the name of the President.

Emergency Powers: The emergency powers of the Indian President are provided by the Part XVIII, Articles 352 to 360, of the Constitution has given such powers. He enjoys such powers once he declares the state of emergency.

Emergency are of three types:

1. Due to the wars and external aggression or internal disturbances

2. Emergency due to the failure of constitutional machinery in the state;

3. Financial emergency.

If the President feels that the security of India is under attack by the foreign forces or war or above mentioned circumstances he can declare the emergency. In such conditions the President becomes very authoritative which means he takes over the administration of the nation and he rules the nation. When he declares the emergency the President converts the federal constitution into unity, can append the Fundamental Right of citizens of the entire nation or part thereof at the time of emergency. The President has to work according to the authority of the Parliament and acts by the advice of the Cabinet. Every claim of the emergency should be put before the Parliament and President cannot be in force more than two months unless otherwise, or at a maximum of six months can be in force.

Nature of the President: The status of the President is almost similar to that of the British monarch. President is considered as the nominal head of the nation, but in reality the Prime Minister is the head of the government, hence the President has to exercise powers under the restriction of the constitution. The President has executive duties under the Article 53. Article 73 states that, "other Ministers shall be appointed on the advice of the Prime Minister." With this it can be observed that in reality the President has no option to select the Council of Ministers, hence, it cannot appoint any one of the President's choice. The Article 74, clearly says that, the President shall in doing functions, act according to the advice of his Council of Ministers and the Prime Minister, The position of the President after 44th Amendment Act, has no authority excluding in some of minimal cases to act discretion.

Provisions of the Constitution: Until the 42nd Amendment Act in 1976, there was suspense over the written provisions of the Constitution, it was about the powers of the President was fixed under the Articles 53(1), 74(1), 75(2), and 75 (3). According to the Article 53(1), says that, "executive power of the Union is vested in the President and shall be exercised by him in accordance with the Constitution." The Article 74(1) says that, "There shall be a Council of Ministers with the Prime Minister at its head to aid and advice the President,"which means that the President has to act according to the advice of the Council of Ministers. The Article 75(2) says that, "The Ministers shall hold office during the pleasure of the President." And the same Article in the clause says that, "The Council of Ministers shall be collectively responsible to the people." And the same Article gives the President authority to dismiss the Council of Ministers. Though there are restricted powers to the President, the status of President cannot be considered as nobody, the Article 74(1), gives authority to ask the Council of Ministers to reconsider the advice given to him. Article 78, makes it clear that President has important authority such as, the important duty of the

Prime Minister to convey all the decision of his Government regarding the administration. Though the President has to act on the advice of the Council of Ministers it does not mean that President has to accept every advice.

President Secretariat: The President has its own secretariat . The Secretary can be regarded as the connecting link between the President and the Council of Ministries- Department of the Government of India (GOI). A Military Secretary will also be working with the President. He is accountable to all ceremonials, management of the President's estate and arrangements for the tours of the President, catering, household and hospitality.

Making Of The Indian Constitution

Prime Minister of India

Introduction:

The Prime Minister is an important figure in the government, he actually administers the administration of the country. The Article 74(1), of the constitution provides that, "there shall be a Council of Ministers with the Prime Minister at the head to aid the President in the exercise of his functions."The status of the Prime Minister has been strengthened further under the 42nd amendment, by making it obligatory for the President to act by the advice of the Council of Ministers with Prime Minister as the head, and occupies a significant position in the constitution and Parliament. The makers of the Constitution intentionally chose the British model of Parliamentary democracy and Prime Minister is the real executive. The Prime Minister of India is almost equal to the President of the USA in the form of Presidential system. It is evident that the Prime Minister is the final arbiter of policy and final repository of real powers in the Parliamentary government.

Election of the Prime Minister: The appointment of the Prime Minister is just like a formality, and President has no discretion in this regard and he shall invite the leader of the majority party in the Lok Sabha to from the Government. Hence, President appoints the Prime Minister, in such cases if there is no clear majority in the Parliament the President might have some sort of priority in appointing the Prime Minister and even in such situations as well he has to call the person who has the maximum support of the members in the Parliament. In case the Prime Minister dies while in the office then President may immediately appoint a caretaker Prime Minister on the grounds of the seniority of the Cabinet Ministers as the Radha Kirishnan appointed Gulzarilal Nanda in 1964, and in 1966, or he may appoint any person from the majority in Lok Sabha like in 1984, Zail Singh appointed Rajiv Gandhi.

Tenure: The tenure of the Prime Minister to be in the office is five years. After the completion of this period again Parliament goes for fresh elections. The Prime Minister lives in the office during the 'pleasure' of the President, it looks as if President can dismiss the Prime Minister whenever he feels like and that type of serious step can be taken only in very rare cases, as soon as he dismisses the Prime Minister he has to appoint a new Prime Minister. The Prime Minister receives Rs.1, 20,000 as monthly salary including all allowances.

Powers of the Prime Minister: There are several powers to the Prime Minister and as the head of the Union Government the Prime Minister does a number of important functions which has been written in the Constitution of India.

Power to form the Government: As soon as the appointment of the Prime Minister takes place the next important duty is to form the Government. The Prime Minister has the authority to pick his own Council of Ministers. Accordingly, Prime Minister selects persons from the Lok Sabha and can choose from the Rajya Sabha members as well. These powers are due to the fact that the Prime Minister is the leader of the party in majority in the Lok Sabha. After choosing the list Prime Minister will submit it to the President for the approval, it looks like that the final powers to appoint the Ministers lies with President but in reality President will have very meagre powers in this regard. Eventually, President has to approve the list submitted by the Prime Minister and he has the power to include or remove from the list anyone's name, the responsibility of the Prime Minister is to form the Government and must have the different interest, communities and real involvement and that is the reason in the Indian Government Muslim and Sikh will have representation. The Ministers will be in the office by the pleasure of the Prime Minister. After forming the ministry Prime Minister has to allocate the business to the Ministers that is portfolios to them and it is the responsibility of the Prime Minister and he has the powers to shift any one from one department to the other department. The Prime Minister being the chairman of the cabinet, summon the meetings and preside during such meetings, when any of the Ministers resigns then the post falls vacant but in cases when the Prime Minister dies in the office then Ministry will be dissolved. Technically speaking the Prime Minister is the connecting link between the President and the Cabinet, but the Ministers can have access to the President individually concerning their departments. Any significant changes in the cabinet or any policy matters for such things must go through the Prime Minister. The Prime Minister in fact has overall responsibility of all the policies of the Government hence, Prime Minister has the powers to supervise all the departments.

 MAKING OF THE INDIAN CONSTITUTION

Coordinator of the Administration: Prime Minister can be considered as the head of the government and the administration, and accountable for the formulation and implementation of the policies of the government, in doing so it is the responsibility of the Prime Minister to supervise all the departments of the different ministries and coordinate the works with them. In fact it is not possible for the Prime Minister to check all the departments for this reason, the different committees of the cabinet looks after such duties, while doing such works by the committees they will consult the Prime Minister. If at all any differences arises among the ministers then Prime Minister solves or sorts out the differences.

Link between Cabinet and Parliament: The Prime Minister is regarded as the connecting link between the Cabinet and the Parliament, and is the main person to deliver his views and speech in the government, all the important announcements about the government and its policies will be addressed by the Prime Minister, and also safeguards the members or ministers of his party during the discussions in the Parliament.

Patronage Powers: The Prime Minister of India has very wide-ranging powers of patronage, all the significant appointments which are made by the President are actually by the recommendation of the Prime Minister,.

Prime Minister and Council of Ministers:

The Prime Minister is the head of the government and also the real executive of the Indian system. Although the Prime Minister is appointed by the President, no system of appointment is given in the Constitution. However, as a convention, the leader of the largest party in the parliament becomes the Prime Minister.

The Appointment of the Prime Minister and the Council of Ministers

- No direct election to the post of PM: The President designates the head of the greater party or the alliance of gatherings that orders a greater part in the majority in Lok Sabha as Prime Minister

- If a single party or alliance does not achieve a majority, the person with the best chance of gaining majority support is picked by the President

- The Prime Minister's term is not fixed. As long as he is the head of the majority party or coalition, he remains in power

- Following the Prime Minister's appointment, the President appoints other Ministers on the Prime Minister's advice

- Ministers can be chosen by the Prime Minister as long as they are members of Parliament. A person who is not a member of Parliament can sometimes be appointed as a Minister. However, within six months of being appointed as Minister, such a person must be elected to one of the Houses of Parliament

Powers of the Prime Minister

The Prime Minister's and ministers' powers, as well as their relationships, are not well-defined in the Constitution. However, as the government's leader, the Prime Minister has broad powers, including the ability to:

- He is in charge of chairing Cabinet sessions and coordinating the work of various Departments

- In the event of a conflict between Departments, his decisions are final

- He exercises general supervision of different ministries

- All ministers work under his leadership

- The Prime Minister assigns work to the ministers and redistributes it

- He also has the authority to remove ministers from office

- When the Prime Minister resigns, the entire cabinet resigns as well

- The de facto commander-in-chief of the armed forces, the prime minister is the most powerful person in India

- In recent decades, the Prime Minister's powers in all parliamentary democracies across the world have grown to such an extent where parliamentary democracies are frequently referred to as Prime Ministerial governments

Council of Ministers

The authority name for the body that exercises executive authority in India. The council of ministers consists of Cabinet ministers, the ministers of state, and other ministers of lower ranks. The Prime Minister leads the Council of Ministers.

- The Council of Ministers normally consists of 60 to 80 Ministers of various grades. Given below are different grades of ministers included in the council of ministers

- Cabinet Ministers are usually top-ranking members of the ruling party or parties in control of key ministries. Cabinet Ministers typically gather to make decisions on behalf of the Council of Ministers. The inner ring of the Council of Ministers is hence the cabinet

- Smaller Ministries are generally in control of Ministers of State with independent charge. They only attend Cabinet sessions if they are specifically invited

- Pastors of State are entrusted with helping Cabinet Ministers and are expected to do so

- As it is impractical for all ministers to meet regularly and debate everything, parliamentary democracy is also known as the Cabinet form of government. Decisions are made in cabinet sessions

- The Cabinet is always supposed to work like a team: Even if the ministers may have different opinions, everyone has to own up to every decision of the Cabinet. No minister is allowed to openly criticize any decision taken by the government even if it concerns another Ministry or Department

Removal of the Council of Ministers

There are many reasons which can lead to the removal of the Council of Ministers. Here are the reasons that can lead to their removal;

- Death

- Self-resignation

- Dismissal by the president for a minister's unconstitutional acts

- After being directed by the judiciary for violation of any law

- If ineligible to be a member of the parliament

- If a vote of a no-confidence motion is passed in the Lok Sabha or the lower house of the parliament

Cabinet Secretariat

- Secretaries, who are civil servants, work in every ministry. The secretaries give the ministers the required background knowledge to make judgments

- The Cabinet Secretariat assists the Cabinet as a whole. Many senior public workers are involved in this as they endeavour to coordinate the operations of various ministries

Conclusion

We can conclude that the Prime Minister of India is the head of the executive branch of the central government. He is the presiding member of the Council of Ministers of the head of the federal cabinet. The prime minister is in charge of selecting and dismissing any member of the cabinet. The prime minister is also in charge of allocating posts to members within the government.

The Council of Ministers is the body that exercises executive authority in India. It consists of various grades of ministers. The Council of ministers consists of Cabinet ministers, the minister of states. The smaller executive body called the Union Cabinet is in charge of taking decisions and hence, the supreme decision-making body of India.

Prime Minister as the Leader of the Lok Sabha:

The Prime Minister acts as the leader of the house of the chamber of parliament—generally the Lok Sabha—they belong to. In this role, the Prime Minister is tasked with representing the executive in the legislature, announces important legislation, and is further expected to respond to the opposition's concerns.

Prime Minister's Secretariat: The office of the Prime Minister is known as the Secretariat, it came into the presence on 15th August 1947. Till 1977, it was known as the Prime Minister's Office, It connects the Prime Minister and Ministers, President, Governors, Chief Minister and Foreign delegates. And on the other hand it relates with party matters, personal correspondence, grievances for the public, etc. The main function is to help the Prime Minister in the routine duties as the head of the government, liaison with ministries, President, etc.

Council of Ministers

Introduction:

The Article 74(1) states that "there shall be a Council of Ministers with the Prime Minister as its head and to aid and advise the President in the exercise of his functions." But after the 42nd amendment in 1976, the Article 74 (1) reads as, "there shall be a Council of Ministers with the Prime Minister as its head and to aid and advise the President in the exercise of his functions and act in accordance with such advice." This Article says that the Prime Minister shall be appointed by the President and Ministers shall be appointed by the President on the advice of the Prime Minister.

   Making Of The Indian Constitution

Council of Ministers and the Cabinet: "The Cabinet is one of the typical anomalies of the British Politics." It came into existence because of the historical situations and conventions and it is considered as an extra constitutional organization. The Cabinet has been rightly pronounced as, "The steering wheel within the Council of Ministers." Every Minister may not be the member of the cabinet, and when he is offered the position of the minster then it will be clearly said that minister is a cabinet rank or not and if the minister is of the cabinet rank then only minister can attend the Cabinet meetings otherwise he cannot attend such meetings but they can attend or other persons can be invited to such meetings as special guests for that occasion. The Cabinet is considered as the highest organization in performing the administration of the country in a democratic manner. Council of Minister's prepares the policies of the government and supervises all the administration. Cabinet is accountable for all final decisions, direction coordination and govern the administration.

Council of Ministers

Article 74 and **Article 75** of the Indian Constitution deal with the Council of Ministers. **Article 74** mentions that the council will be headed by the Prime Minister of India and will aid and advise the President. Article 75 mentions the following things:

- They are appointed by the President on the advice of Prime Minister

- They along with the Prime Minister of India form 15% of the total strength of the lower house i.e. Lok Sabha. (The number cannot exceed 15%)

- 91st Amendment Act provided for the disqualification of the minister when he stands disqualified as a member of Parliament. (Difference between Lok Sabha and Rajya Sabha can be referred to in the linked article.)

- A Minister ceased to exist as one if he is not a member of either house of Parliament for six consecutive months.

- Parliament decides the salary and allowances of the council of ministers.

Is the advice tendered by the Council of Ministers' binding on the President?

Yes, the advice is binding on the President and this provision was introduced by the 42nd Amendment Act 1976 and 44th Amendment Act

1978. The acts also mentioned that the advice given by the council cannot be inquired into by any court. Read about the 42nd Amendment Act and the 44th Amendment Act in the linked articles given below:

- 42nd Amendment Act
- 44th Amendment Act

Collective Responsibility of the Council of Ministers

In England, the Cabinet system is based on conventions. The framers of our Constitution considered it fit to incorporate the system in the Constitution. The principle of collective responsibility finds a place in Art. 75(3) where it is stated that the Council of Ministers shall be collectively responsible to the Lok Sabha. In other words, this provision means that a Ministry which loses confidence in the Lok Sabha is obliged to resign. The loss of confidence is expressed by rejecting a Money Bill or Finance Bill or any other important policy measure or by passing a motion of no-confidence or rejecting a motion expressing confidence in the Ministry. When a Ministry loses the confidence of the Lok Sabha the whole of the Ministry has to resign including those Ministers who are from the Rajya Sabha. The Ministers fall and stand together. In certain cases, the Ministry may advise the President to dissolve Lok Sabha and call for fresh elections.

Types of Ministers

The Indian Constitution does not categorize ministers into ranks, however, in practice seen in India, ministers are of four types:

Cabinet Ministers—He is present and he participates in every meeting of the Cabinet.

Minister of State with independent charge—He is a Minister of State who does not work under a Cabinet Minister. When any matter concerning his Department is on the agenda of the Cabinet, he is invited to attend the meeting.

Minister of State—He is a Minister who does not have independent charge of any Department and works under a Cabinet Minister. The work to such Minister is allotted by his Cabinet Minister.

Deputy Minister—He is a Minister who works under a Cabinet Minister or a Minister of State with independent charge. His work is allotted by the Minister under whom he is working.

Deputy Prime Minister:

The Deputy Prime Minister of India is the second-highest ranking minister of the Union in the executive branch of the Government of India and is a senior member of the Union Council of Ministers. The office holder also deputises for the prime minister in their absence.

The office has since been only intermittently occupied, having been occupied for a little more than 10 years out of the 75 years since its inception. Since 1947 India has had 7 deputy prime ministers, of which none having at least one full term. The first was Vallabhbhai Patel of the Indian National Congress party, who was sworn in on 15 August 1947, when India gained independence from the British Raj. Serving until his death in December 1950, Patel remains India's longest-serving deputy prime minister. The post was vacant until Morarji Desai became the second deputy prime minister in 1967 and has the second-longest tenure. Morarji Desai and Charan Singh were the deputy prime ministers who later became Prime Minister of India. Jagjivan Ram and Yashwantrao Chavan became deputy prime ministers consecutively without the break in different ministries. Devi Lal is the only deputy prime minister to represent both parties in the same post. Lal Krishna Advani was the seventh and last person to serve as the deputy prime minister of India until the post became vacant.

Size of the Cabinet: Article 75 (1) of the Constitution of India states that the total number of Ministers, including the Prime Minister, in the Council of Ministers must not exceed 15% of the total number of members of the Lok Sabha. Though there is a maximum limit, there is no minimum number of ministers who must be part of the Cabinet.

The size of the Cabinet is dependent on a variety of factors like political compulsions, representation of various factions, mode of functioning of the Prime ministerial candidate, experience and capabilities of ministers etc. In some situations like formation of a coalition government, it is inevitable that the Cabinet be relatively large so that all the parties that form the coalition are represented. While a reasonable sized Cabinet proves effectual due to splitting of and equal sharing of responsibilities, a large Cabinet results in chaos. There are only a limited number of ministries for the Ministers to oversee, and it would be a classic case of too many cooks spoiling the broth if too many ministers are put in charge of smaller ministries. There would be overlap of duties, and differences between the different ministries, overcoming which will be a challenge in itself. These issues will occur even if there is a very capable Prime Minister, and hence, must be avoided.

Functions of the Cabinet: The cabinet of India is mostly similar to that of British cabinet with regard to some of the functions, but there are certain functions which can be performed by Indian cabinet only.

Executive Powers: The executive powers are given by the Constitution to the President who actually performs on the advice of the Council of Ministers, in fact these executive powers of the Union Government is actually done through the Council of Ministers. The Cabinet issues the directives to the State Governments as well. They formulate the policies of the Union Government and they implement in a proper manner in the country, the policies such as national, international level.As soon as they make the policy they perform through their respective ministries and Ministers will be in charge of one or more than one departments. The matters which are regarded as routine are decided by the Minister itself but the policy matters are to be decided by the Council of Ministers.

Legislative Powers:

Amendment to the Constitution — The Cabinet is instrumental in planning and moving the Amendment to the Constitution.

Summoning the Houses of Parliament — Although the Houses are summoned by the President, initiative in this matter is taken by the Ministry of Parliamentary Affairs.

Issuing Ordinances — Cabinet also advises the President to issue ordinances when the Parliament is not in session.

Financial Powers:

Budget — The Finance Minister prepares the Annual Budget containing estimates of income and expenditure for the ensuing year.

1. Though the budget is passed by Parliament, usually no changes are made in the budget figures against the wishes of the Cabinet.

2. Any amendment to the budget proposals against the wishes of the Cabinet that may be passed by the Lok Sabha amounts to a vote of No-Confidence in the Ministry. It happens only when the Ministry has lost the support of the majority in the Lok Sabha. In such a situation the Ministry must resign.

Finances of the Government — The Cabinet is responsible for the expenditure of the government for presenting the demand for grants and also for raising necessary income by various means including taxation.

 MAKING OF THE INDIAN CONSTITUTION

Introduction of Money Bills — A Money Bill can be introduced in the Lok Sabha only by a Minister.

Control over the Appointments: All the important appointments which are to be taken by the President under the Constitution such as, Attorney-General, Union Public Service, Chief Election Commissioners, etc. are done by the President on the recommendations of the Council of Ministers.

Foreign Relations: The Council of Ministers decides all the foreign policy of India and also suggests what kind of policy and relation India must have with other nations.

Relationship with President: The executives at the Union Government are the Council of Ministers. According to the constitution all the executive authority has been given to the President, who can do it either directly or through the subordinate officers and the Council of Ministers. The 42nd amendment has given the authority to the Council of Ministers to advice the President. The former President, VV Giri, stated about it as, "Our Constitution in 1976 makes an explicit provision compelling the President to act in accordance with the advice of the Ministers who continue in the office during the President's pleasure. If this provision continues to exist even, now, and the people want it that way, it will be in the fitness of the things to go in for a presidential form of Government, as otherwise this office becomes a drain on the public exchequer." During the Janata Government the amendment in the Constitution granted the President the right to refer back matter to the Council of Ministers for one time, but the advice by the President is reconsidered by them then President has to approve it. Hence the actual executive power lies with the Council of Ministers and President has to act upon it. The President cannot dismiss a ministry which has the support of the majority members, the President cannot remove any one unless he was advised by the Prime Minister to do so.

Relations of Council of Ministers and Parliament: The relations between the Parliament and Council of Ministers is friendly and very close. The Constitution says that to become Minister one must belong to any of the House, if he is not the member of the House at that time then he needs to seek the election form either of the house within six months and if he fails to do so then loses the ministry. All the members of the Council of Ministers are collectively responsible to the Parliament according to the Constitution. Parliament can regulate the Council of Ministers in various manners such as, Parliament can pass no-confidence motion against one or the entire ministry to resign; it cannot accept the Bill introduced by the ministry, it can pass or reject the bills introduced by the opposition to which the Council of Ministers differ; in case of the no-confidence motion the ministry need not resign, it advises the President to dissolve the Parliament for fresh elections. The Parliament can bring the weakness and shortcomings of government by the way of questions, supplementary questions, adjournment motions, etc.

Extraordinary Functions: In the extraordinary time the Cabinet exercises the functions like **'sui generis'**, hence, the President has the authority under Article 352 to makes laws by an ordinance during the recess of the Parliament, but in fact these ordinances are made by the Cabinet and advices President to propagate them. Likewise, Part XVIII of the Constitution has given the powers to Cabinet to advise President to proclaim the emergency in such conditions when it is required. Whatever activities performed by the President during the emergency in reality it is done by the cabinet.

Supreme Cour and Judicial Review

Introduction:

The most important part of the federal constitution is the division of powers of the government among the Centre and the State Governments. It is definite that everyone in the country follows the laws made by the Parliament, but some challenges a law as they regard it unjust, inappropriate and strict; others violate it because of the mindset they have and affinity to act like the way of criminal. The Constitution of India provides to act like a guardian of the Constitution, and this Court is the highest authority in the country and only one court of such kind in the country.

Composition of the Supreme Court: When the Supreme Court in 1950, came into existence according to the Constitution, then it had 8 judges. The Supreme Court is comprised of Chief Justice and the Judges. The number of Judges can be increased or can be decreased by making an Act in the Parliament. The number of Judges were increased to 17 in 1977, excluding the Chief Justice. The number of the judges has been increased to 25 in the year 1986, excluding the Chief Justice, and the number of Judges increased to 30 in the year 2009, excluding the Chief Justices. Hence, the numbers of total judges in the Supreme Court presently are 31 which include the Chief Justice. The Supreme Court is in New Delhi.

Appointment of the Chief Justice: The Chief Justice is appointed by the President of India in discussions with the Judges of the Supreme Court and the High Court in the different States of the country, and the judges are appointed by the President in consultations with the Chief Justice of India. An ex-Judge of the Supreme Court may also be asked to act as a Judge of the Supreme Court by the Chief Justice. There is also a provision that the 'Acting' Chief Justice can be appointed.

Qualification to be a Judge: To become the Judge of the Supreme Court a person must have these qualifications:

1. Must be a Citizen of India;

2. Must have been a judge of High Court or two or more such courts in succession for a period of five years at least;

3. Must have been the advocate of High Court or two other such court at least for 10 years;

4. Must be, in the opinion of the President of India, an eminent jurist; Every Judge while holding the office, has to take an oath.

Tenure of the Judges: There is no minimum age recommended for the appointment of the Supreme Court Judge. According to the Article 124, any Judge of the Supreme Court can hold office until he attains the age of 65 and after attainment of such age he retires and gets the pension as fixed by the law. There are limitations on the practice while in the office, the article 124 (7), says who has held the offices that, "No person who has held office of a judge of the Supreme Court shall plead or act in any Court or before any authority within the territory of India." But he can be asked by the Government to perform such kind of work.

Removal of the Judge: A judge of the Supreme Court can be removed from his office by an order of the President. The President can issue the removal order only after an address by Parliament has been presented to him in the same session for such removal.

The address must be supported by a special majority of each House of Parliament (ie, a majority of the total membership of that House and a majority of not less than two-thirds of the members of that House present and voting). The grounds of removal are two—proved misbehaviour or incapacity.

The Judges Enquiry Act (1968) regulates the procedure relating to the removal of a judge of the Supreme Court by the process of impeachment:

No judge of the Supreme Court has been impeached so far.

Impeachment motions of Justice V Ramaswami (1991–1993) and the Justice Dipak Misra (2017-18) were defeated in the Parliament.

Establishment: The Constitution of India has provided the Supreme Court to have its own establishment and to have a total control over it. All the appointment such as, officers and servants are made by the Chief Justice, the conditions and other things will be decided by the Supreme Court only. The salaries, maintenance and other financial requirements are met by the Consolidated Fund of India. The Article 129, says that, Supreme Court shall be a Court of Record and shall have all the powers of such a court including the power to punish for contempt of itself, Which means that all the record of the court must be kept and can be called as evidence when required.

 Making Of The Indian Constitution

Immunities and Contempt Proceedings: There is full independence to the judges of the Supreme Court, no one can discuss regarding the conduct, decision of the Judge in the Parliament and no bad motives can be ascribed to the Judge nor the decision of the Judge can be criticized in both the Houses, Whereas the Supreme Court has power to start contempt proceedings against any person who tries to influence the judges.

Powers of the Supreme Court: The Supreme Court has more powers than any other federal court, the Constitution has provided original, appellate and advisory jurisdiction to this Court.

Original Jurisdiction: The Supreme Court has original jurisdiction in any dispute

- Between the Government of India and one or more States;

- Between the Union Government and any state or States on the one side and one or more other State on the other; or

- Between two or more States. The disputes among the above mentioned parties law or facts which are brought to the Supreme Court, out of any treaty, agreement, covenant, engagement and such other things entered into.

The views of the High Court's have to be decided by the Supreme Court.

Appellate Jurisdiction in Civil Criminal Matters: The Article 133 says about it, the appeal can be made to the Supreme Court from any judgment, decree or final order given by the High Court, it can hear the appeals from the decisions of High Court on both civil and criminal matters.

The jurisdiction for appellate has two features

1. Jurisdiction to hear appeal in civil and criminal matters or proceedings which involve the interpretations of the constitution and

2. Jurisdiction to hear the appeals in other civil and criminal matters.

The Article 134 says that, an appeal shall lie to the Supreme Court from any judgment, final order or sentence in a criminal case of High Court in the territory of India. In the civil matters an appeal lies to Supreme Court against the judgment of High Court, and if such Court certifies that the case is fit for appeal to the Supreme Court. It can give special leave to appeal against any judgment, decree, sentence or order, made by any tribunal or court in India. It is important to note that Supreme Court has no right to grant leave to appeal against judgment of military court or tribunal. Whereas in Criminal cases, an appeal can be made against the judgment of High Court, to the Supreme Court if:

1. The High Court has in appeal reserved an order of acquittal of an accused person on sentence to death; or

2. The High Court has withdrawn for trial before itself any case from any court subordinate to its authority and has in such trial convicted the accused person and sentenced to death; or

3. The High Court certifies that the case is fit for appeal to the Supreme Court.

Appeal by Special Leave: According to the Article 136, the constitution provides Supreme Court for regular appeals of the High Court decisions. Writ Jurisdiction: According to the Article 32 gives powers to Supreme Court to issue directions or orders or writs such as **Habeas Corpus, Mandamus, Prohibition, Quo Warranto and Certiorari** of the Fundamental Rights.

Advisory Jurisdiction: The article 143 says that "if at any time it appears to the President that a question of law or fact has arisen or is likely to arise which is of such nature and of such public importance that it is expedient to obtain the opinion of the Supreme Court upon it, he may refer the question to the court for consideration and the court may, after such hearings as it thinks fit, report to the president its opinion thereon." The President asked the Supreme Court for its opinion on many occasions.

Court of Record: The Supreme Court can be considered as the court of records, and have all the powers which includes the power to punish for contempt of itself. Court of record means that, the acts and judicial proceedings are recorded and cannot be challenged when present before any court for evidence.

Power to Review its own Judgement or Order: According to the Article 137, the Supreme Court has powers to review its own judgement or orders, it can be done under these conditions such as, identification of new facts; mistake or evident on the face of the records; and any other sufficient reasons.

Guardian of the Constitution: Supreme Court is the guardian of constitution, the final authority to interpret the constitution given to Supreme Court. It is the accountability of the Supreme Court to supervise

     Making Of The Indian Constitution

that both the Centre and State Governments works under the provisions made by the Constitution. For this reason it has the authority to review the laws passed by the legislature and orders issued by the Executive, has the power to claim it as unconstitutional if they contradict to any provision of the Constitution. Supreme Court has the power to make and examine the disputes regarding the elections of President or Vice President of India and the decision of the Supreme Court is final in this matter. If the Supreme Court declares the chairman or the members of UPSC, of guilty of misbehavior then President can remove them.

Judicial Reviews of Supreme Court: The strength and dignity can be best controlled from its authority of Judicial Reviews of the Supreme Court. The authority of the Supreme Court is that it can review the laws passed by the Legislature and orders issued by the Executive, has the power to claim it as unconstitutional if they contradict to any provision of the Constitution. The Constitution of India has given the powers to Parliament and the States to formulate the legislations according to the limitations. If Supreme Court observes that they have crossed the limitations then it can interfere in it and has the authority to declare it as unconstitutional. The Judicial Review does two important functions such as,

1. Legitimizing the action of the government; and

2. To safeguard the Constitution from any undue encroachment of the government.

The Fundamental Rights, which includes the rights to constitutional remedies, spread the field of Judicial Reviews to the Fundamental Rights as well, the Article 12 and 13, save the rights from attack by either the executive or the legislature through laws already in force or the laws formulated from now. The legislations of executive such as, ordinances, orders, regulations etc., will not be permitted to encroach on these rights. Chief Justice Kania witnessed in the case, **V. K Gopalan vs The State of Madras** in 1950, by which the "The inclusion of Article 13 (1) (2) in the constitution appears to be a matter of abundant caution. Even in their absence, if any of the Fundamental Rights was infringed by any legislative enactment, the Court has always the power to declare the enactment to the extent it transgresses the limits, invalid. The law declared as ultra vires of the Constitution by the Supreme Court is binding on all the courts within the territorial limits of India and the subordinate courts cannot apply the void law."

The Article 21, says that, "No person shall deprived of his life and personal liberty except according to the procedure established by the law." The absence of the phrase 'due process of law', limits the power of the Indian courts, the judiciary of India has no freedom to bring their own conception of justice and equality to the judicial interpretations like that of Supreme Court of USA. The liberal attitude of the courts in India, is seen and they limit their own liberty of actions, it has been held by the courts that they are guaranteed to prompt words of the constitution and not the essence of the Constitution. At the same time courts are not prepared to restrict their power on the grounds of the Constituent Assembly debates. The Parliament overpowered the limitations obligatory on the power regarding the amendment and curtailed Fundamental Rights by the 24th Amendment, the rights of the Supreme Court are limited by this act and to declare a law affecting Fundamental Rights under the Articles 14, 19, and 31 as void, and the law is passed to effect the Directive Principles under the Article 39 (a) or (c). These amendments had lot of disagreements and were challenged in the Court, the Fundamental Rights Case of 1973 or **Keshavanand Bharati case.** Finally the Court accepted that law passed to give Directive Principles under article 39 (b) or (c) could not be challenged so far they did not affect the basic structure of the Constitution. Indian Constitutions safeguards judicial review of legislation such as Articles 13, 32, 131, to 136, 143, 226, 251, 254 and 372.

Provisions for the Weaker Sections

Introduction:

There is total differentiation between the Law and Order of the State and the Welfare of the State, and in the recent times most of the governments are giving priority to the welfare of their citizens. If we observe the Indian history from the ancient times it was noticed that all the rulers were very much fond of welfare of their citizens, they had provided all such amenities of welfare to them, such as planting the trees on the road sides, building of roads, making temporary stay homes or shelters to the travellers even they had the arrangements for the posts, etc. In those days the main attention was with the mechanism of defence and to bring peace in the country without such wars. It was the year in 1929, when the 'Great Depression' occurred in United States of America was considered as the main reason for new thoughts, it made the people to rethink about the new ideas so that a change can be seen in the society. This led to new thinking in United States of America, a new thought of 'liberalism' in Britain and such thought of 'socialism' in Russia were the most significant developments in the world and later developed into the new ideas for the welfare of the community. After the Second World War the countries which favored the wars and being capitalists altered their ideas and brought a new look to it by adopting and creating a State consisting of welfares for their citizens. In fact the communist ideology brought such ideas in them, though the Communist Party has seen its decline in the 1990s in Russia and other East Europe countries, still the concept of liberalism, democracy and other ideologies are still vibrant and alive.

The concept of social welfare which consists of social security to the community and welfare of the community. When the Constituent Assembly made the Constitution of India, the ruling party Congress had such thoughts to implement programmers which benefits the community, they decided to have policies like liberal, democratic and welfare of the society in India. The consequences of such thoughts resulted in paving the way to assure equality and justice to every citizen, was laid in the Constitution which came into force on 26th January, 1950. The constitution consists of Fundamental Rights and entire chapter of Directive Principles and with the latest amendments socialism was included to the preamble and the Directive Principles were justifiable and compulsory.

The Article 38 talks about this, "that State shall strive to promote the welfare of the people by securing and protecting, as effectively as it may, a social order in which justice, social, economic and political shall inform all the institutions of the national life." In other words, we can understand that the Constitution of India is mainly grounded on the principles of social, justice and the social equality of the community.

The Article 46, is one of the most important in the Constitution of India, because it talks about the welfare, it says that, State has to give a special care education and the economic interest of the weaker section of the people in the country and with special attention for Scheduled Castes, and Scheduled Tribes. Along with this, it also says about the rights of minorities of religious and linguistics are mentioned very clearly to safeguard their interests. It also talks about the welfare of the women and child development, and handicapped and disable. With the guidelines which are provided in the Constitution for the welfare, under the Social Security, Employee's State Insurance Scheme, Family Pension, Legislations on Labour, Safety of the Workers etc., are included, while under Social Welfare, the schemes for the upliftment of the depressed and disable sections such as, Scheduled Castes, Scheduled tribes, Backward classes, Minorities, Physically and other such challenged, Pensioners, Prisoners and other such schemes for Rehabilitation and Prohibition.

Administrative Arrangements: Though there are several ministries to take care of the welfare of the weaker sections, they took some changes with regard to the administration so that these welfare schemes would reach the needy section of the people, for that reason it was on 25th September 1985, it combined subjects such as, Welfare of the Scheduled Caste and Scheduled Tribe and Socially and Economically Backward classes and Other Backward Classes (OBC) they have included the linguistic and religious minorities which were under the Home Ministry; to tackle the needs of welfare of disabled and physically challenged, to rehabilitate those who are drug addicts, juvenile maladjustments, welfare for the aged; and the administrative matters of Wakf, which was under then Ministry of Law, but on 26th April, 1990 it was shifted to the Department of Welfare, and now these Ministries, reorganized into the Department of Welfare and Department of Women and Child Development. The Welfare Ministry is the nodal agency for all the activities, planning the policies, implementing and coordinating such programmers effectively so that it can reach those weaker sections of the society.

These departments can be seen at Centre and State levels, they have their own interests and purposes, and it can be observed that the setups for the purpose of administrations will be different in States, these States plan according to their requirements. In the States of Andhra Pradesh, Bihar, Madhya Pradesh and Odisha they have separate departments to take care of the Tribal Welfare, Minorities, and Backward Classes. But in other States, they have committees of the members of the Legislatures on the guidelines of the Central Parliamentary Committee. In the States of Tamil Nadu and West Bengal they have Tribal Advisory Committees, for the welfare of the Scheduled castes. It is the main responsibility of the Union Government to formulate such welfare policies in the country and coordinate such schemes through the State Governments.

Scheduled Caste and Scheduled Tribe Welfare: The new Constitution came into force on 26th January 1950, and later the Preamble resolved to constitute India into a Sovereign Socialist Secular Democratic Republic, which gives the assurances to its citizens on Justice, Equality, and Fraternity. The Constitution of Part III, on Fundamental Rights assures all its citizens of the Right to Equality and the Right to Exploitation, under the Part IV, Directive Principles of the State Policy also provides such rights, under the Article 46, included some other provisions for the upliftment of the weaker sections of the society. The Hindu society which created 'untouchables', are educationally backward and economically as well, M.S Srinivas a sociologist called them as 'intermediate class'.

To the constitution by adding clause (4) to Article 16 which gives for equality of opportunity in public employment. The Article 46 demands the safeguards and promises promotional, educational and economic interest of "the weaker sections of the people", along with reservations in public services and these classes need to have the reservations in technical education which are provided by most of the State Governments. The article 46 of the Constitution talks about the welfare of Scheduled Caste and Scheduled Tribes and other weaker sections such as Backward Classes and Minorities. The main responsibility of the Governments in providing education, and economic development of these weaker sections of the society, the Union and State Government are very much dedicated and firm in implementing such schemes for the sake of the weaker section of the people, for this they have kept their political agendas aside. Even after the starting of such measure for them still their condition is not up to the mark the Scheduled Caste and Tribe have undergone number of atrocities and to overcome such atrocities Union Government has enacted SC, ST Prevention Act 1989, it came into force on 30th January 1990. The Parliamentary Committees have been started to guarantee such activities by the Union Government in 1966, 71 and 73 Amendment Act to study the programme implementation for SC and STs in the country. This Commission comprises of a Chairman, Vice-Chairman and five other members who are appointed by the President. The Commission has given individual powers to control itself. It submits the report to the President about the effectiveness of welfare programmes in the States, depending upon their report the Union Government enquires the reasons from the States. The Commission was given the powers and it acts like Civil Court. The important functions of the Commission are as follows:

1. It examines, regulates and coordinates all the matters regarding guarantees given by the law and to appraises the working of guarantees.

2. It assures the rights of the SC and STs and also looks into the complaints about their deprivation.

3. It implements and guides on the planning methods of the socio-economic developments of SC and STs and assess their development

4. It reports to the President annually about the working of these assurances to them and it also suggests changes in it.

5. It also works with regard to the welfare and other developmental programmes for them

6. It works as a consultant. The Central and State Governments consults the Commission on all important policy matters for the benefit of SC and STs. Along with government the other NGOs involve in such activities and Government provides financial support to them.

The Union Government has taken some other steps under the Article 350 and 352 of the Constitution, reserved the seats for Lok Sabha and State Legislatives for a period of 10 years initially, and it extended by 62nd amendment for another ten years. There are no reservation seats in the Rajya Sabha. The Article 335, gives that the claim of Scheduled Caste and Scheduled Tribes must be taken into regard to maintain the efficiency of the administration. State Governments also formulated rules to give them powers by item 41 of the State List of the 7th Schedule for reservation

  MAKING OF THE INDIAN CONSTITUTION

of the posts for them and took further measures to bring them into the mainstream and to increase the representation in the State Services.

Welfare of Other Backward Class: In the Indian community the society has been divided on the grounds of the caste hierarchy of descending order. It is very unnatural that large number of people which were the resultant of such caste division falls under the lower caste and performs menial jobs and other such works. And these classes are always under the deprivation and considered as the 'untouchables' because of the work they do in the society. Because of such caste division and untouchables Hindu society gave birth to new religions like Jainism, Buddhism and Sikhism. Even in the Hindu society one can see there are sects such as, Brahmo Samaj and Arya Samaj. In the recent years Gandhi and Ambedkar fought for this cause. The domination of caste can be very clearly seen in the southern parts of India, and there were many such movements to control such atrocities. In the year 1920, there was a movement against it which was led by the E.V Ramaswamy Naicker, in the Madras presidency which consists of present states of Tamil Nadu, Andhra Pradesh, Karnataka and Kerala. The result of this movement came into existence in Madras, and it started a movement against the upper class oppression and won the battle by entry into Hindu temples and reserving high position in government as well. This movement was against the Brahmins, Hindi and Sanskrit, and this party in the coming years became Dravid Kazagam, then Dravid Munnetra and finally as Al-India Dravid Munnetra Kazagam Party. The Congress party which fought for the freedom of the country under the leadership of Mahatma Gandhi, was against such caste domination and untouchability, and it was fortunate that the Constitution was made under the guidelines of Congress.

Women Welfare: There are welfare schemes for the benefit of the women and children as well, before it was under the Ministry of Social and Women's Welfare and this ministry has become Department of Women and Child Development and it is shifted to the Welfare Ministry. This new Department came into existence on 26th April 1990. In this Department there is a separate bureau known as **The Women's Development Bureau.** It has the main functions to perform, to look after the welfare and developmental programmes of women in the country and it makes the policies, plans and programmes which are necessary for their upliftment at present juncture. It also looks after enacting, implanting and the needed legislations pertaining to women. The important contributions of this Bureau are here under:

Legislative Measures: The most important achievements are number of law amended and at the same time enacted for their sake. It was due to its efforts, in 1956, Immoral Traffic Prevention Act, the original Suppression of Women and Girls Act, 1956 was amended in 1978 and later 1986; 1961 act on Dowry Prohibition, was amended in 1984; 1986 Act, of Indecent Representation 87 of Women (Prohibition) the commission of Sati Prevention Act, 1987; and it also worked for many such amendments and criminal laws, offence of rape, domestic violence, etc. which are made punishable under the Indian Penal Code.

The Central Social Welfare Board: It comes under the Companies Act of 1956. It has developed many programmes for the welfare of women, children and physically challenged persons. This board gets the financial assistance from the Department of Women and Child Development and NGOs. This welfare board looks after welfare services with regard to women, it provides financial assistance to those NGOs who work under it. It has number of activities such as inspection, assessment and statistics along with field counselling. It also undertakes construction of complexes, quarters for staff, strengthening State Social Welfare Advisory Boards, the implementation of socio-economic programme with aim to provide women particularly economically backward, the destitute, widows and deserted and needy, it also provide women with opportunities for work and wages. It also concentrates those areas where income-generating is possible and inculcate habit among the women about this.

Other Important Programes: The other most important programmes for the upliftment of women are starting of Women's Development Corporation, Employment and Income Generating Production Units, Short Stay Homes, Hostels for working women, Rehabilitation and Training Centers. The most important achievement of this board is the National Commission for Women, under the Act 1990 to provide representation of women in all areas and to check discrimination against women, redressal of grievances. The most important function of this Commission is to study and monitor all matters pertaining to constitution and legal guaranties given for women, it also takes grievances and takes notice on suo-motu, and takes actions against deprivation of women's rights. The welfare policy was started for SC and ST's from the beginning in 1950's, but in the case of backward sections the new policy for the upliftment educationally and economically started in 1993 only.Government has established several financial organizations to give financial assistance to

     Making Of The Indian Constitution

the backward communities. Out of these policies for them the policy to provide special educational opportunities is working due to fact that their political and cultural identities have an impact in the process of democracy. It is necessary to tackle their day to day problems with the help of local administration.

Conclusion: There is total differentiation between the Law and Order of the State and the Welfare of the State, and in the recent times most of the governments are giving priority to the welfare of their citizens. It was the year in 1929, when the 'Great Depression' occurred in United States of America was considered as the main reason for new thoughts, it made the people to rethink about the new ideas so that a change can be seen in the society.

After the Second World War the countries which favoured the wars and being capitalists altered their ideas and brought a new look to it by adopting and creating a State consisting of welfares for their citizens. In fact the communist ideology brought such ideas in them, though the Communist Party has seen its decline in the 1990s in Russia and other East Europe countries, still the concept of liberalism, democracy and other ideologies are still vibrant and alive. On 25th September 1985, it combined subjects such as, Welfare of the Scheduled Caste and Scheduled Tribe and Socially and Economically Backward classes and Other Backward Classes (OBC) they have included the linguistic and religious minorities which were under the Home Ministry; to tackle the needs of welfare of disabled and physically challenged citizen. The article 46 of the Constitution talks about the welfare of Scheduled Caste and Scheduled Tribes and other weaker sections such as Backward Classes and Minorities.

The main 88 responsibilities of the Governments is providing education, and economic development of these weaker sections of the society. The Union Government has made amendments for their benefit and commissions for SC and STs, other Backward Classes along with National Commission for Women to look after the needy women for the development.

Reviewing the Constitution - Sarkaria Commission

Introduction:

The Constitution of India predicts two-tier government, which means one Federal Government and the Governments at all State levels. The State

Governments have some limitations and Union Governments supervises them.In most of the cases, they need to have cooperation among them. The Union Government may be regarded as the supreme authority and it controls most of the activities of States, hence, for certain reasons have to depend on the Central Governments for assistance. For these reasons there are some sort of struggles and problems in the relations of the Centre and State relations. If such strains and problems continue for long time between them, then there would be a danger for the integrity and the unity of the Nation.

Appointment of the Commission: It is evident that such problems must be sorted out as early as possible so that there will be an agreement and cooperation is required for the smooth running of the Governments at the Centre and the States. To sort out these problems, in March 1983, the then Prime Minister of India, Indira Gandhi, declared in the Parliament about the proposal to appoint the Commission to study and suggest recommendations in this regard. The Commission was headed by the retired Supreme Court Judge, R.S Sarkaria. Indira Gandhi stated about the Commission in the Parliament as, "The Commission will review the existing arrangements between the Centre and the State while keeping in view the social and economic developments that have taken place over the years. The review will take into account the importance of unity and integrity of the country for promoting the welfare of the people." She also said that, "The Commission would examine the working of the existing arrangements between the Centre and the State and recommend such changes in the said arrangements as might be appropriate within the present constitutional frame." The Government of India on 9th of June 1983, established this Commission under the Ministry of Home Affairs notification **No. IV/11017/1/83-CSR,** dated June 9, 1983. Ministry appointed two others, B. Shivaraman on 7th July, and Dr. Sen on 27th July 1983, as the members of this Commission.

Commission's Terms of Reference: The Commission's terms of reference in the notification as pronounced were: "The Commission will examine and review the working of the existing arrangements between the Union and States in regard to powers, functions and responsibilities in all spheres and recommend such changes or other measures as may be appropriate. In examining and reviewing the working of the existing arrangements between the Union and States and making recommendations as to the changes and measures needed, the Commission will keep in view the social and economic developments that have taken place over the years and have due regard to the scheme and framework of the Constitution which the founding fathers have so sedulously designed to protect the Independence and ensure the unity and integrity of the country which is of paramount importance for promoting the welfare of the people."

The Report of the Commission and Main Contents: In the year 1988, the Commission gave its report and it was published, it mainly consisted of two parts,

1. The main report and

2. The State Governments and other political parties, send memoranda to the Commission. The Commission has examined the main issues such as, direct attitude on Centre-State relations particularly on legislative and administrative aspects and also the requirement for starting a standing Council on Centre-State relations under the Article 283 of the Constitution, to assure their relations, and also talked about such related issues like, the role of Governor, Emergency Provisions, Deployment of Union's Armed Forces in the State to regulate the law and order situation, Reservation of State Bills for attention of the President and it also mentioned about the All India Services. The Commission also examined the relations of the Centre and State pertaining to the socio-economic development activities which includes, Economic and Social Planning, Financial Relations, National Economic and Development Council and assorted matters such as, Agriculture and industry related matters, Inter-State trade and commerce, Inter-State river disputes, mines and minerals, food and civil supplies, forests, and mass media, etc. were very closely examined and suggested recommendations by the Commission so as to rectify such problems and by giving priority to the welfare of the country.

Centre-State Relations and Important Concerns: The important issues regard to the centre and state relations are as follows:

1. The Commission when it reviewed the different States and political parties which submitted memoranda, observed that there are different views and most of them are of the opinion that the framing of the constitution is good and it must not be disturbed or changed, but at the same time some of them are of the opinion that, it has to be changed and it needs radical changes so that it fulfil their own views of the federal structure.

2. Most of them opined that Central Government has taken the control over all aspects or centralised all its programmes and the State Governments are, diminished to simple administrative organizations of the centre.

3. Most of them opined that, Centre is taking most of the amount of the concurrent list, giving very less to the states. They stated that legislation is more often than not, assumed with no or insufficient discussion with the states.

4. The idea behind the institution of Governor as a connecting link between Centre and State Governments. It is viewed that the Governor has been used to destabilize the state governments, particularly of those parties which are different in the power at the Centre, imposition of President's rule, prevention of many state bills which are reserved for President's consideration.

5. It is opined that, the states resources have not developed at the same rate when compared to the responsibilities of the state, they have also argued that more resources to be pooled in so that state governments can share, if required by amending Constitution.

6. Another important concern is the occurrence of planned development which has concentrated all authority with Centre, the Planning Commission is also part of Central government. They recommended that restructuring of Planning Commission is needed and to restrict the interference of Centre in this regard.

7. The system of controls, licences and permits has flourished to sub-serve the needs of a planned regime. This led to great extension of power and authority to the Central Government when compared to the State Governments and local bodies, this type of system is pleaded and needs to be revised.

8. It is also stated disorganizations or forums which are predicted in the constitution for sorting out problems arising in the working of Centre State relations, (e.g., Permanent Inter-tate Council as contemplated in Article 263) have not been created at all. When dispute between Centre and State Government arises, the Centre must not be both the disputant and judge but case must be examined by independent evaluator before taking such decision. The relations between them must be worked out in such a manner of cooperative federalism and consensus in all the areas of common interest.

 MAKING OF THE INDIAN CONSTITUTION

The Important Recommendations of the Commission: The Commission has suggested some important recommendations to sort out the problems between them, keeping welfare of the Nation. The main recommendations are as follows:

Legislative Relations: The recommendations about the relations with regard to legislative relations are:

- The residuary authority of the legislation concerning taxation must be in the Concurrent List and it should be remain there, and the residuary matters apart from the taxation must be kept in the Concurrent List and for this reason the constitution may be suitably amended.

- In the large interest of the Nation, the Centre has to subjugate only that ground of concurrent subject on which uniformity of policy and action is needed, and by so it has to leave the remaining and details for State action within the broad framework of the policy laid down by the law of the Centre. Whenever Centre proposes for the legislation in such times it has to consult with States individually and also in groups, with the Inter-Governmental Council. A resume of views of the State Governments and the comments of the Council must accompany the Bill when it is introduced in the Parliament.

- Whenever the State passes a resolution in the State Assembly for the formation or the abolition of Legislative Council in the State is received, the President shall cause the resolution to be placed, within a reasonable time, before Parliament together with the comments of the Central Government. Parliament thereafter can accept or reject the demand enclosed in the resolution.

If the resolution is passed in the Parliament then central Government shall introduce required legislation for its implementation. 13.6.2 Administrative Relations: There are serious complaints to the Articles 256, 257 and 365 with regard to the relations of the Centre and State, the Article 256, says that, the executive power of every State shall be so exercised as to ensure compliance with the laws made by Parliament and the Article 257 says that, the executive powers of every State shall be so exercised as not to impede or prejudice the exercise of the executive power of the Union, and in both cases the executive power of the Union shall extend to the giving of such directions to a State as may appear to the Government of India to be necessary for the purpose. The Article 365, says that, if a State fails to comply with or give effect to, any directions given by the Union Government, it shall be lawful for the President to hold that a situation has arisen in which the Government of the State cannot be carried on in accordance with the provisions of the Constitution. The commission embraces that the Articles of 256, 257, and 365 are healthy provisions, intended to protect the management between the Union and States for the effective implementation of Union laws and the Policies of the country specified therein. At the same time it mentions that direction under Articles 256, 257 and the request of approvals under the Article 365, highest caution must be exercised and all prospects explored for resolving opinions of conflict by all other existing means.

Deployment of Union Armed Forces in the State: The Commission opined that, there is no need to change any Union laws with regard to the relationship among the Union Armed Forces and the State Civil authorities. But the union Government can deploy their forces only on the request from the State authorities, it very mush required to consult State Government before deploying them.

All-India Services: Commission considered the All-India Services as a necessity even today because it is the premier organisation for maintaining the unity and integrity of the country. Any move to break up the All-India services or to allow any State to choose out of the scheme should be considered as reversing and harmful to the larger interest of the country. They opined that, the All-India Services should be strengthened and greater stress placed on the role expected to be played by them.

Inter-Governmental Council (Article 263): The President has empowered to establish inter-Government Council under the Article 263, and to define the nature and functions to be performed by the organisation and the method. Such forum has not been established. The Commission suggested that a permanent Inter-State Council, called the Inter- State Council (IGC), must be started under the Article 263 and the council must be with the following functions which are given in Article 263: 95 "Investigating and discussing subjects in which all of the States, or the Union and one or more of the States, have common interest, or making recommendations upon any such subject and, in particular, recommendations for the better coordination of policy and action with respect to the subject". The Commission further suggested that the Zonal Councils which were contained under the State Reorganisation Act, 1956 should constituted afresh under Article 263. 13.6.10 Financial Relations: The Commission has examined much detailed study on the relations of the Centre- State relations pertaining to the present financial relations among them and they have made many suggestions in this regard. The income generating out of the taxation from the agriculture is an important issue, both the Union and State Governments are not ready for alter in the provisions of the constitution. It stated that, the question of raising resources from this source by forging political consensus and the modalities of levying that tax and collection of proceeds etc., would needed in depth and complete consideration in the National Economic and Development Council. Another important recommendation of the Commission is by the amendment of constitution proceeds, Corporation Tax, must be made permissibly sharable with the States if and as Parliament by law so provides. So that the revenue of the States would have greater constancy and certainty in future. The Commission has made number of suggestions for the development of the working of the Finance Commission, The Planning Commission and the National Development Council. It also suggested that the division of responsibilities between Finance Commission and Planning Commission is good and may be continued. The Commission stressed the need of decentralization of the planning process. It observed that "Since there is a general tendency towards greater centralization of power there is a special need in a country like India for a conscious and purposive effort to counter it all the time. There is considerable truth in the saying that undue centralization leads to blood pressure at the Centre anemia at the periphery. The inevitable result is morbidity and inefficiency. Indeed, centralization does not solve but aggravates the problem of the people". The Commission observed that there is no need to be drastic changes in the constitution, though there was a request for the change in the constitution. On this observation Commission observed that, "the working of the Constitution in the last 37 years, has demonstrated that its fundamental scheme and provisions have withstood reasonably well the inevitable stress and strains of the movement of a heterogeneous society towards its development goals. The Constitution has been amended a number of times to adjust to its working to the changes in the environment. "In our view, it is neither advisable nor necessary to make any drastic changes in the basic character of the Constitution". "But there is certainly scope for improvement and reform in a number of aspects. The actual working of the Constitution leaves much to be desired". 13.7 Conclusion: The Constitution of India predicts two tire government, which means one Federal Government and the Governments at all State levels. The State Governments have some limitations and union Governments supervises them in most of the cases, they need to have cooperation among them. To sort out these problems, in March 1983, the then Prime Minister of India, Indira Gandhi, declared in the Parliament about the proposal to appoint the 96 Commission to study and suggest recommendations in this regard.

The Commission was headed by the retired Supreme Court Judge, R.S Sarkaria. In the year 1988, the Commission gave its report and it was published, it mainly consisted of two parts,

1. The main report and

2. The State Governments and other political parties, send memoranda to the Commission. The Commission has examine the main issues such as, direct attitude on Centre –State relations particularly on legislative and administrative aspects and also the requirement for starting a standing Council on Centre- State relations under the Article 283 of the Constitution, to assure their relations, and also talked about such related issues like, the role of Governor, Emergency Provisions, Deployment of Union's Armed Forces in the State to regulate the Law and order situation, Reservation of State Bills for attention of the President and it also mentioned about the all India Services.

Constitutional Review Commission

Introduction:

Since the enforcement of the Indian Constitution on 26th January, 1950 the amendments were made to the original text eighty times and these occurred in bit and pieces manner whereas the amendments to the 42nd and 44th have been considered as the most complete ones. In 1971, there was a talk about producing a comprehensive refit of the Constitution formed during general elections during the battle of power. They put efforts to bring socio-economic change rather than bringing required changes in the Constitution and the socio-economic changes applied the brakes to do so. The Constitution of India predicts a two-tier government, which means one federal government and one government at state levels. The State Governments have some limitations and Union Governments supervises them in most of the cases, they need to have cooperation among them. The Union Government may be regarded as supreme in authority and it controls most of the activities of States. The first ever Commission on review of Constitution, though on the relations of Centre-State relations, the Government of India on June 9th 1983, appointed a Commission by the then Prime Minister Indira Gandhi, under the Chairmanship of RS Sarkaria, a retired Supreme Court judge and the Commission submitted a report in 1988. The most important Commission to study the entire structure of the Constitution and to recommend its views about the Constitution was the Review Commission. It was established to review the Constitution of India in the light of the developments since independence. The NDA government went ahead and constituted the National Commission to review the working of the Constitution (NCRWC or the Review Commission hereafter), and the Commission was constituted under the Chairmanship of Justice M.N. Venkatachaliah, a retired Chief Justice of the Supreme Court of India and a former Chairman of the National Human Rights Commission.

Formation of the Commission:

In the years 1970s and 1980s there were discussions about the Presidential type of government in India, the influential personalities from the political arena, people from the academic area, and the media had very strongly campaigned for making an executive authority, which will be autonomous of daily parliament control, which means that a type of structure, mostly similar to the United States Presidential form, and estimated that this would be the solution for all the problems of the governance in India. From the mid-1980s to 1990s the discussions about the comprehensive review about the Constitution was subsided, but it again reappeared overall as an election subject for diverse reasons. After 1995, no party had been emerged with a simple majority to form the government in the Lok Sabha elections, this actually gave rise to successive efforts by dissimilar groups of political parties to form a stable government. From 1995 to 1998 the people of India had witnessed governments which could not stay for five years tenure, the games which resulted in general elections and fall of the Deve Gowda and IK Gujral governments in a very short span. The other reason was the lack of enthusiasm of the major political parties to ally with the right wing, nationalist, Bharatiya Janata Party (BJP) and try to repair the damage formed the governments, but unfortunately they could not run the government for a full term of five years for such reasons and the result was the dissolution of the Lok Sabha and fresh elections were called for. In the year 1998, the BJP- led government formed in those general elections fell because of the intrinsic illogicality of coalition politics and the game played by the opposition parties. But in the later general election in 1999, the BJP led National Democratic Alliance (NDA) with an understanding with 24 such political parties formed the coalition government in the

Centre. In that election BJP did not contest with its manifesto but it give out a National Agenda which were discussed with its allies which had minimum common points in it which includes the arguing of article 370? The manifesto of NDA did not mention about the Commission to review the Constitution of India or to examine the consequences which arose since Independence. But the NDA government on 26th October, 1999 comprised the issue of the review of the Constitution in the joint session which was addressed by the President RK Narayan. This gave a clear picture that NDA wanted to find out a factual solution to end the problems due to the coalition politics, and making such amendments to clear the long problem and also to know the performance and whether it still had the importance or it need to be amended accordingly, of the 50-year-old Constitution of India. The address mentioned that, "A Commission comprising noted constitutional experts and public figures shall be appointed to study a half-century's experience of the Constitution and make suitable recommendations to meet the challenges of the next century.Government will also examine replacing the present system of no-confidence motion by a system of "Constructive Vote of Confidence" and a fixed term to the Lok Sabha and the Vidhan Sabhas (Legislative Assemblies in the States), in order to prevent political instability both at the Centre and in the States." In spite of the public manifestation of uncertainties by the President of India afterwards, the NDA led government went to start the National Commission to review the working of the Constitution (NCRWC), it was otherwise called as Review Commission. The NDA Government justified the setting up of the Commission within 24 hours issuing the official notification on 22nd February, 2000. It also gave the reason for it by saying, there are interruptions present among the actual successes of the country and the inventive objectives of the Constitution even after fifty years of Independence and it was required to bond the breach. On the event of annual Presidential address during the budget session , the president's address reads, "The Constitution which India adopted fifty years ago has served us well. It has been a reliable guarantor of the Parliamentary democracy, secularism and fundamental rights which all of us cherish.

It has also inspired the spread of the democratic consciousness in our society, empowering dalits, adivasis, backward classes and women and making our system governance more participatory and progressive. While keeping the basic structure and salient features of the Constitution inviolate, it has, however become necessary to examine the experiences of

     Making Of The Indian Constitution

the past fifty years to better achieve the ideals enshrined in the Constitution. The government has therefore, set up a broad-based Constitution Review Commission. The recommendations of this Commission will be presented before Parliament, which is the supreme decision-making body in Indian democracy. A very hot discussion about the Review Commission, during the budget session took place in the Parliament. It was most significant to note that the NDA Government did not move the resolution about the setting up of a Constitutional Review Commission in the Parliament, but it delivered the executive order for setting up National Commission to Review the Working of the Constitution (NCRWC).

Appointment of the Commission:

By the executive resolution in the Parliament, the National Commission to Review the Working of the Constitution (NCRWC), was set up on 22nd February 2000, by the Department of Legal Affairs, Ministry of Law, Justice and Company affairs. The resolution mentions that, the government agreed to set up the Review Commission to fulfil its pledge contained in the President's address to the joint session of the Parliament after the constitution of the 13th Lok Sabha in October 1999.

Terms of Reference of the Commission:

The Department of Legal Affairs, Ministry of Law, Justice and Company Affairs issued the resolution, and it consists of the terms and references to the Commission like: "The Commission shall examine in the light of the experience of the past fifty years, as to how best the Constitution can respond to the changing needs of efficient, smooth and effective system of governance and socio-economic development of modern India within the framework of Parliamentary democracy and to recommend changes if any, that are required in the provisions of the constitution without interfering with its basic structure or features."

The Review Commission stated that there was a requirement to maintain and strengthen the Constitutional provisions so that it can lead to the upliftment of the living conditions of the poor and deprived and assure them with sufficient means of livelihood. It also understood that the Constitutional Rights of the Scheduled Caste, Scheduled Tribes and other Backward Classes and the Minorities should be efficiently safeguarded and upgraded. The Commission also mentioned that it will examine the working of the present provisions in the Constitution, laws applicable, and practice and consider how better these goals may be attainable. The government resolution states that the Review Commission will complete its work and make its recommendations to the government within a period of one year by March 2001.

Composition of the Review Commission:

The Commission is comprised of a Chairman, and ten members, apart from a Secretary and an administrative and research staff.

Chairman of the Review Commission: Justice M.N Venkatachaliah is appointed as the Chairman of the Review Commission, he was a retired Chief Justice of Supreme Court, and former Chairman of the National Human Rights Commission.

Members of the Review Commission:

1. Justice B.P. Jeevan Reddy, Former Judge of the Supreme Court and currently the Chairman of the Law Commission of India.

2. Dr. Subhash C. Kashyap, Former Secretary General of the Lok Sabha and the author of several books on constitutional and electoral reforms. He is appointed as the Secretary of the Review Commission.

3. Justice R.S. Sarkaria, Former judge of the Supreme Court and the Chairman of the Sarkaria Commission on Union-State Relations.

4. Justice K. Punnayya, Former High Court Judge.

5. Dr. Abid Hussain, Retired Diplomat and a Former Ambassador to the United States of America, UN special rapporteur on the freedom of expression. 101 101 6. P.A. Sangma, Former Speaker of the Lok Sabha and a Former Chief Minister of Meghalaya, member of the thirteenth Lok Sabha from the Nationalist Congress Party.

6. Soli J. Sorabjee, Attorney-General of India.

7. K. Parasaran, Former Attorney-General of India.

8. C.R. Irani, Managing Director and Editor-in-chief of the newspaper, The Statesman.

9. Ms' Sumitra G. Kulkarni, Former Member of Parliament. The Commission has submitted its report on 11th March 2002 to the Prime Minister of India.

Sources

1. A.P. Avasthi, Indian Political System, Lakshmi Narain Agarwal, Agra, 2005.

   MAKING OF THE INDIAN CONSTITUTION

2. J.C. Johari, Indian Government and Politics. Vishal Publications, Delhi, 1989. 3. DD.Basu, Introduction to the Constitution of India, Prentice-Hall India, New Delhi, 1998.

3. JC. Johan, The Constitution of India, A Politico-Legal Study, Sterling Publishers Private Ltd. New Delhi,2005,

4. Dr.J.N.Pandey, The Constitutional Law of India, Central Law Agency, Allahabad, 2013.

THE END

9 789355 849830